SECOND EDITION

I'm on LinkedIn—Now What???

A Guide to Getting the Most OUT of LinkedIn

By Jason Alba

HappyAbout.info

20660 Stevens Creek Blvd., Suite 210
Cupertino, CA 95014

Trademarks

Warning and Disclaimer

Praise for this Book

"I was ready to abandon my LinkedIn account before I read Jason Alba's concise and remarkably useful guide. Jason writes with remarkable clarity, provides one useful tip after another about how to use it most effectively, and unlike so many users guides that offer breathless and uncritical hype, Jason candidly explains the virtues and drawbacks of LinkedIn's features. Beyond that, Jason has such deep experience with the web that the book contains hundreds of broader lessons about how to get the most of the web: I learned an enormous amount from this little gem."
Robert Sutton, Stanford Professor and author of The No Asshole Rule

"Jason offers a unique perspective on networking that's of interest to anyone that is a job seeker, entrepreneur, or networking enthusiast. He has been all of these and his experiences with LinkedIn enable him to offer an integrated review for anyone to make the most of the LinkedIn tool. His book is a reflection of his deep understanding of people, technology and change in the market and can easily save the average new user months of time in trial and error."
Nadine Turner, Six Sigma Black Belt

"If you are new to LinkedIn, you are in for a treat when you read 'I'm On LinkedIn—Now What???' If this book were available the first year LinkedIn started, it would have helped LinkedIn to be better understood and would have helped thousands of professionals get the most out of LinkedIn."
Vincent Wright, Chief Encouragement Officer, MyVirtualPowerForum.com

"In an age of social networking, LinkedIn remains one of the best for business people. Mr. Alba gives a wonderful first-hand insight on the how-to's of using the service: this guide has been a long time coming. I am delighted that he's taken the time to put together, in a single volume, how to get the best out of the service."
Jack Yan, CEO, Jack Yan & Associates, JackYan.com

Author

- Jason Alba, http://ImOnLinkedInNowWhat.com
  LinkedIn Profile: http://linkedin.com/in/jasonalba

Publisher

- Mitchell Levy, http://happyabout.info
  LinkedIn Profile: http://linkedin.com/in/happyabout

Executive Editor

- Scott Allen, http://theVirtualHandshake.com
  LinkedIn Profile: http://linkedin.com/in/scottallen

Cover Designer

- Cate Calson, http://CalsonGraphics.com
  LinkedIn Profile: http://linkedin.com/in/calsongraphics

Layout Designer and Copy Editor

- Teclarity, http://Teclarity.com
  LinkedIn Profile: http://linkedin.com/e/fpf/2002741

v

Dedication

To Kaisie, Samantha, William, Taylor and Kimberly.

Acknowledgments

No one told me that I would have to do a second edition only a year later—I guess that's what I get for writing a book about a technology that can change so quickly. Thank you to the LinkedIn team, who continues to change the product, making a second edition so necessary!

I got considerable strength and encouragement from many friends and acquaintances I've met since I got laid off almost three years ago. To the thousands of people who have purchased the first edition, thank you. Your comments on my blog (ImOnLinkedInNowWhat.com), your emails, and evangelizing my book have encouraged me to keep this work current.

I have a close circle of associates and partners who have been instrumental in giving me feedback, advice, and tips to help me hone my message and delivery, and make sure that what I present is just what their professional and executive clientele needs.

My publisher deserves a big hat-tip, as he encouraged me, challenged me, and believed in me during the last 18 months. Thank you Mitchell and HappyAbout, for the opportunity to change my life and career path by becoming one of your authors.

Finally, deep gratitude and respect goes to my family, immediate and extended, as I have seen them support my entrepreneurial dream, wondering what exciting thing is coming up next while enjoying the road we are on.

A Message from Happy About®

Thank you for your purchase of this Happy About book. It is available online at http://happyabout.info/linkedinhelp.php or at other online and physical bookstores.

- Please contact us for quantity discounts at sales@happyabout.info
- If you want to be informed by email of upcoming Happy About® books, please email bookupdate@happyabout.info

Happy About is interested in you if you are an author who would like to submit a non-fiction book proposal or a corporation that would like to have a book written for you. Please contact us by email editorial@happyabout.info or phone (1-408-257-3000).

Other Happy About books available include:

- I'm on Facebook—Now What???:
  http://happyabout.info/facebook.php
- Twitter Means Business:
  http://happyabout.info/twitter/tweet2success.php
- Collaboration 2.0:
  http://happyabout.info/collaboration2.0.php
- The Emergence of The Relationship Economy:
  http://happyabout.info/RelationshipEconomy.php
- Internet Your Way to a New Job:
  http://happyabout.info/InternetYourWaytoaNewJob.php
- Blitz the Ladder:
  http://happyabout.info/blitz.php
- Happy About My Resume:
  http://happyabout.info/myresume.php
- Happy About LinkedIn for Recruiting:
  http://happyabout.info/linkedin4recruiting.php
- Tales From The Networking Community:
  http://happyabout.info/networking-community.php
- Scrappy Project Managment:
  http://happyabout.info/scrappyabout/project-management.php
- The Home Run Hitter's Guide to Fundraising:
  http://happyabout.info/homerun-fundraising.php
- 42 Rules of Marketing:
  http://happyabout.info/42rules/marketing.php
- 42 Rules of Social Media for Business:
  http://www.happyabout.info/42rules/social-media-business.php
- 42 Rules for Driving Success With Books:
  http://42rules.com/driving_success_with_books/

viii

C o n t e n t s

Figures

Foreword by Bob Burg

Several years ago I began receiving requests from friends, inviting me to join a new online membership site called LinkedIn. Soon I was getting emails from people I barely knew, asking me to "join their LinkedIn network." Although I'd been using the Internet for networking and relationship-building for some time, I really wasn't all that interested in LinkedIn. Still, not wanting to hurt these people's feelings, I accepted.

I went through the process of posting my Profile, but didn't do much with the site. As time went on, more and more people sent me invites.

Every so often, I'd be asked for help connecting someone with someone else, who apparently knew someone who knew someone I knew. From time to time, people from specific groups who'd read my book, 'Endless Referrals'[1] would notice I was a LinkedIn member and ask me to contribute an article for their newsletter. I guess you could say I'd become a part of the LinkedIn community. Yet still, I wasn't really utilizing LinkedIn in any active or significant way.

Why not? No perceived need, and no desire. (You might remember those two reasons from Sales Training 101 as the two most common reasons prospects say "no.") And why didn't I have any perceived need or desire? Because I had frankly no idea what to do or how to make LinkedIn a positive experience for me.

---

1. Bob Burg, 'Endless Referrals,' McGraw Hill, 2005

That's exactly where this book comes into play. Jason Alba has done a first-rate job of solving that challenge for me, and he will for you, too.

A former unemployed IT professional and business strategist, Jason found that finding a good job, even in a "job seeker's market," was a pretty daunting task. Today, he runs a career management company, called JibberJobber. In *'I'm on LinkedIn—Now What???'* he presents us with an actual system to tap into the power of the LinkedIn service.

And that's the key word here: system. That's what I was lacking in my early LinkedIn experiences.

Why is having a system so important? I define a system as, "The process of predictably achieving a goal based on a logical and specific set of how-to principles." In other words, if it's been proven that by doing A you'll achieve B, then you know that all you need to do is follow A and you'll eventually achieve B. As Michael Gerber points out in his classic, *'The E-Myth Revisited'*[2] (slightly paraphrased): "Systems permit ordinary people to achieve extraordinary results...predictably."

Whatever the B is you want to achieve here, *'I'm on LinkedIn—Now What???'* provides you with the A for getting it. After an excellent introduction explaining exactly what LinkedIn is and how it (basically) works, Jason then walks you through a guided tour of clear principles and powerful strategies for getting the most out of your LinkedIn experience.

---

2. Michael Gerber, *'The E-Myth Revisited,'* HarperCollins, 1995

While Jason sees LinkedIn as an excellent business-building tool, he also looks at the site with a carefully critical eye. Jason himself began achieving great success utilizing LinkedIn only after floundering with it his first few months, and he does not hold back in pointing out its weaknesses and suggesting areas where LinkedIn could improve and make its service more valuable for its members. And I found especially refreshing those passages where he points out the areas of LinkedIn where he has still not grasped its highest use. Someone that humble, I tend to trust.

Jason tells us that LinkedIn is not a replacement for your networking efforts (online or offline); rather, it is an excellent tool for facilitating some facets of your networking strategy. I absolutely concur. The creed of my Endless Referrals System®[3] is that, "All things being equal, people will do business with, and refer business to, those people they know, like and trust." And no computer or online medium is going to replace that personal connection—but it certainly can enhance it and provide potential networking contacts with more opportunities to connect. In this book, you'll learn how to do exactly that, whether it's for direct business, resources you need, helpful information, finding joint venture partners, hiring a new employee, or getting hired for a new job.

Something I particularly appreciate about Jason's approach is that he shows us not only how we can gain value from LinkedIn but, just as importantly, how we can utilize LinkedIn to provide value to others. As any true networker

---

3. http://www.burg.com

knows, this is not only immensely satisfying in its own right, but it is also the best way to receive even more value oneself.

As you travel through this excellent guide, be prepared to learn from a man who has done his homework. Jason has learned what he knows the hard way, through trial and error, both his own and many other peoples', and put it all between the covers of a book so that you and I can learn it all the easy way!

Best wishes for great success,

Bob Burg
Author of 'Endless Referrals' and coauthor of 'The Go-Giver'

Part I
Getting Started

Part I is all about getting started on LinkedIn.

- Chapter 1 talks about my personal experience with getting started, and why I decided to write this book.

- Chapter 2 talks about what LinkedIn is and isn't, which is critical to understand since so many people are expecting one thing and see something totally different.

- Chapter 3 is a crash course on your Profile, and what you need to do to set it up correctly.

- Chapter 4 talks about setting up your Account & Settings so your interaction with the website reflects your needs.

1 Introduction

As I went through the first edition of this book with a fine-toothed comb, I realized there was a lot of room for improvement in the second edition. My understanding of networking, technologies in the social networking space, and LinkedIn have grown over the last year. Additionally, the LinkedIn company and website have had considerable changes. Many times I thought there was enough to merit another edition, and I know if I just hold on for a couple of months I'll have more stuff to write about. Alas, I have to draw the line somewhere. You can keep up-to-date on the topics within this book at ImOnLinkedInNowWhat.com

I remember when I was first introduced to LinkedIn. It was February 2006 and I was walking out of a networking meeting with a guy who came to tell us he had just landed a new job. As we were walking out, he recommended I create an account on LinkedIn. Of course, I didn't want to because I already had too many accounts with other websites and doubted this would add value to my job search.

I did get an account, and found LinkedIn to be a very lonely place. For the first few months I had only six connections. Searching for valuable contacts (there were about eight million users in LinkedIn when I signed up) produced no results, which led me to believe the search function was broken. I didn't find anyone whom I was interested in contacting (I searched for "manager" in "Salt Lake"), and never received any communication from a recruiter or hiring manager.

LinkedIn just wasn't working for me. I knew if I could just figure out what all the buzz was about, and learn how professionals were using LinkedIn to improve their business and careers, I could benefit. But I just didn't understand what I needed to do.

And so I began to learn what LinkedIn is all about—how to use it, how to benefit from it and what its limits were. Once I began to understand how it was intended to be used, it became much more valuable to me in my personal career management.

As I was learning the hows and whys of LinkedIn I found a lot of people were still confused. It's obvious *why* you would use LinkedIn if you are a recruiter (The first book[4] dedicated entirely to LinkedIn is written specifically for recruiters) or job seeker. But I found people regularly scratching their heads wondering how to use it—even recruiters! As a business owner I've used LinkedIn to bring value to my business. From finding the right contacts to enhancing your brand, LinkedIn has been a great tool for me in my overall social marketing strategy.

I hope this book can serve as a reference on how you can get the best out of LinkedIn. I'm on LinkedIn—Now What??? is not a comprehensive book on networking, nor is it a general book on social networking there are already some great books on these subjects. I'll talk about networking and social networking, borrowing from the experts and using examples from my contacts, many of whom I've met through LinkedIn. By the time you finish this book you should have a solid understanding of what LinkedIn is, how to use it and why things on LinkedIn work the way they do.

Before we jump in, a quick word on why this book is dedicated to just LinkedIn. I don't call myself a social networking expert, and I don't spend all of my time learning about, using and optimizing social

---

4. Bill Vick and Des Walsh, *Happy About LinkedIn for Recruiting*, Happy About, 2006

Chapter 1: Introduction

networks. There are just too many, with too many differences, and things change too rapidly. For example, as of April 2008, Ning, the social networking site that allows you to create your own social networks for free, had over 230,000 different social networks![5] This book is meant to go deeper into LinkedIn, where I believe every professional should have a presence, to help you get more out of LinkedIn than I did in my first few months.

LinkedIn is NOT the only social tool I use. I use Facebook, Twitter, blogs, and Yahoo! Groups to help grow my network, nurture relationships and share my brand. I use these tools as part of a complementary strategy, connecting and participating as appropriate, and moving on to perform my job. I have gotten a lot of value out of my multi-environment strategy, and would not stop using any of these tools to use just one.

Perhaps this book will teach you how to use LinkedIn more effectively. Perhaps you will implement some of this learning to find new business, customers, employers, vendors, partners, employees, or even friends. While there are no guarantees, I know that many people have had their professional and personal lives enriched because of LinkedIn, and hope you can, too!

Now, let's get started!

Chapter Summary

- This book came about because of my own confusion with using LinkedIn.

- LinkedIn is not the only online networking tool you should use, but it is definitely one of the most powerful.

- How you get value out of LinkedIn might be different than how I get value out of LinkedIn, but many of the ideas and techniques shared here should help you get more value out of LinkedIn.

---

5. http://tinyurl.com/ning-fast-company —in the first edition I reported Ning had over 70,000 social networks. That's pretty serious growth! fastcompany.com/magazine/125/nings-infinite-ambition.html

2 What is LinkedIn?

It's critical to understand what LinkedIn is (and later, what it isn't). Depending on who you are and what you need, it may be extremely valuable, moderately valuable, or only slightly valuable. The value you get out of LinkedIn also depends on your time commitment to proactively manage and use its features and capabilities.

Some call LinkedIn a social network, others call it a business network (explicitly stating that it is not a social network), and others call it a contact management system. I agree that it has elements of each, and also agree with the skeptics that it isn't necessarily any of these things.

TIP: LinkedIn is a **tool**. Understanding the value proposition of LinkedIn, and secondary benefits, should help you get the most out of your investment.

LinkedIn is a website where you can find others who you should connect with, so they can add value to you, or you can add value to them, or just because adding each other to one-another's networks seems to make a lot of sense. It is a tool to expand your network, allowing your network to grow wider and deeper.

In addition, you can set up your own Profile so others can find you. Your Profile will have similarities to a resume—you can list where you went to school, where you worked, dates of employment, what your tasks/roles were, what your interests are, etc. You can state what your current interests are (open to job opportunities, interested in hooking up with classmates, etc.), and you can choose what information to make available to other LinkedIn members and what to make available to anyone (even the general public who aren't members of LinkedIn). We'll talk about this later, in the Your Profile chapter.

The value of LinkedIn grows as more people join. Imagine there were only 1,000 people in LinkedIn, and they all lived in one city, and followed one profession. Then, LinkedIn would not be a valuable source of contacts for you unless you happened to live in that city or had an interest in that profession. Fortunately, there are over twenty-eight million people who have created accounts and Profiles on LinkedIn, which means you have a huge database of prospective contacts. But the value doesn't stop at the contacts and their Profiles.

Because of the number of users in LinkedIn, and their diverse back-grounds and interests, it is a place where an immense amount of infor-mation gets shared. One of the stronger commonalities between its members is a desire to have some element of business or professional networking. It is not a site for music bands to advertise (like MySpace is), although musicians do have Profiles. It is not a site to look for dating opportunities, although I'm sure people have hooked up and perhaps even married as a result of relationships forged through LinkedIn. It is a site where people come to develop relationships that can be profes-sionally beneficial.

This means members are a terrific source of knowledge about business and political issues, how-to's, career management, job leads, consulting opportunities and more. LinkedIn does not take advantage of all of the social networking features you see on other sites; however, it provides value beyond just having network contacts.

What LinkedIn Is Not

Currently, LinkedIn is not a social network site where you go to create fun little communities or followings. You can see examples of such sub-communities on sites like MySpace, MyBlogLog, and Facebook. LinkedIn allows you to create your network connections, often see your connections' contacts, and even interact with them through an internal, proprietary mailing system. With regard to social networking features, LinkedIn is not as feature-rich as the other sites, as it doesn't allow users to share blog posts, leave messages and comments on your contacts' Profiles in a conversational way for others to see.

LinkedIn is not a contact manager in the traditional sense of contact management. A contact manager allows me to put contact information in a system and manage data for each contact. For example, I would put the name of a network contact and then update phone numbers, special dates (birthdays, graduations, etc.), spouses name, kids names and ages, etc. In LinkedIn I can only add connections that:

a. are already in LinkedIn (or accept an invitation to join LinkedIn), and

b. agree to connect with me.

In August, 2008, LinkedIn introduced the ability to start entering this type of data for my contacts, but it is very preliminary, and I am not using it yet. Also, if a contact chooses to disconnect from me, would I lose all of my data? It's too early to recommend LinkedIn as a CRM.

This doesn't work for me as a "contact manager" because I meet people all the time who aren't on LinkedIn, won't get on LinkedIn, or for some reason don't care to connect (although I still want to manage information about our relationship). Additionally, if a contact decides to terminate our connection, they are out of my network. Can you imagine a salesperson allowing prospects (contacts) to opt-out of a private prospect list, for no reason?

I think it's a haphazard practice to use LinkedIn as your contact management system when you have so little control over who is actually in your network, what data is collected and managed, and who can see your contacts. At a minimum, calling LinkedIn a contact management tool is a misnomer. If you use LinkedIn as a CRM, make sure you backup your contacts regularly. I wrote[6] about a career coach who mistakenly had her account disabled for a little while, wondering if she would ever get her network back. The account was reinstated, but I think she'll regularly backup her contacts just in case.

While LinkedIn is a networking tool, it is not a networking silver bullet. Timeless networking principles such as "givers-gain," etiquette, long-term relationship nurturing, and investing time and effort in others are critical. LinkedIn is not a replacement for your networking efforts (online or offline); rather, it is an excellent tool to facilitate some facets of your networking strategy.

Finally, LinkedIn is not a time hog. Once you get some initial parameters set up (mostly your Profile and preferences) you don't have to worry about spending much time in LinkedIn. Of course, if you have the time, you can derive additional benefits by using some of the more advanced features such as Answers.

Why do people use LinkedIn?

With over twenty-eight million people in LinkedIn (there were only thirteen million when I wrote the first edition) you are sure to find different strategies, motives and techniques for using LinkedIn. While it boils down to "people meeting people," here are some examples of why people sign up for, or use, LinkedIn:

- **Professionals** - to develop their personal brand; to search for potential clients; to determine job titles and positions of prospects; to research potential contacts.

---

6. http://tinyurl.com/linkedin-maintenance
jibberjobber.com/blog/2008/07/17/linkedin-mainte-nance-do-this-right-now-or-else/

- **Job seekers** - to network; to find new leads and opportunities; to network into a company (do a search on a company and see who in their network might have an in where they want to interview); to establish a presence and hopefully be found by recruiters, hiring managers and HR.

- **Recruiters and hiring managers** - to find prospects for open positions; to develop a rich network of prospective candidates; to search through connections of their connections, digging deeper into second and third degree contacts.

- **Entrepreneurs** - to develop an online presence; to establish a brand; to meet other entrepreneurs or potential business partners, customers, investors, etc.; to build a team of cofounders and employees; to do market research; to get publicity.

There's a nice list at Web Worker Daily[7] that lists "20 Ways to Use LinkedIn Productively." You should list what your own objectives are with LinkedIn. Some of the tactics presented in this book may be appropriate for you while others may trigger ideas to get more out of LinkedIn. Remember, while LinkedIn may be useful to help you do your job, there is always a chance others are looking for you, so be sure to have your Profile as updated as possible.

LinkedIn Benefits

"I'm on LinkedIn—Now What???" That's the question I hear from a lot of people. The most common complaint I hear is based on the idea that people think they are signing up for the "premier professional networking site" and find their experience does not match up to all the hype. I think this is more an issue of training (what is LinkedIn and how do I use it) than technology.

I have strong feelings about social networking—I personally feel "social-networked-out!" I receive email invitations to social networks weekly and wonder why I'm being invited. Sometimes they are geography-based, sometimes they are interest-based—and usually they don't appeal to me (because I don't live in that particular geographic area, or

---

7. http://tinyurl.com/yukjpj
webworkerdaily.com/2007/06/15/20-ways-to-use-linkedin-productively/

don't have much passion for that particular interest!). Many invitations come without the inviter knowing he sent the invitation at all, as invitations may have gone out to his address book, and I was in his address book!

Putting aside the various nuisances of social networking (and some are more annoying than others), it's definitely worth my time to actively participate in LinkedIn. I think about how my job search in 2006 would have been different had I been able to develop a LinkedIn network the size I have now (over 1,000 connections), and how my career management, and even job performance, could have been better if I had a LinkedIn strategy. Here are some of the benefits I see resulting from active participation in LinkedIn:

1. **Ability to be known.** Using LinkedIn, participating in an email forum with other LinkedIn users, commenting on LinkedIn's blog and participating in Answers give you the ability to be known by others who are interested in networking. The ways you participate, including your understanding of netiquette, will help define your personal brand. Contribute, give and share in a positive way and you can develop a good reputation in these communities.

2. **Ability to be found.** It's been said that recruiters will show up where passive candidates are. There are a lot of recruiters who use LinkedIn! Recruiters have books on how to optimize LinkedIn as a tool to find candidates, and you'll find other professionals (like "sourcers") who spend a lot of time on LinkedIn looking for talent. You won't be found if you aren't there (and you won't be appealing if you haven't spent time fixing up your Profile). Whether you are actively looking for a job or not, in today's world there are a bunch of companies called "Me, Inc." (Thank you, Tom Peters!).

3. **Ability to find others.** If you have a network that is "big enough," which LinkedIn indicates is around 65 contacts, you should have sufficient reach when you do searches, to find what you are looking for. I'm amazed when I do searches and come up with certain results. For example, finding someone with the last name of "Jason" who has "Oracle" in their Profile. I was only able to find this person through LinkedIn because I have a network that is "big enough." If I only had 5 first degree contacts, I would not have found Mr. Jason who has Oracle in their Profile.

4. **Opportunity to learn and share.** LinkedIn Answers is an excellent tool and one of my favorite features in LinkedIn. Answers might be the only reason some users log into LinkedIn! Some people have found new business, while others have received expert advice and information faster than any other option available to them.

5. **Ability to connect with Group members.** There are many closed or exclusive Groups that you will have a hard time joining (such as alumni Groups from colleges and universities). LinkedIn has over 90,000 Groups,[8] some of which you might be able to join. When you join a Group you get access to the other Group members. Group memberships can help you get in touch with people who share certain commonalities such as geographic locations, associations, university affiliations, interests, etc.

6. **Opportunity to show you are plugged in to current technology.** Having a LinkedIn account doesn't necessarily brand you as someone smart or technologically hip—but it can help! If you understand LinkedIn (and other tools) to some degree, you can communicate with others about these modern tools and resources. Of course, LinkedIn won't make you smarter than you already are but being able to talk about it intelligently and showing that you have more than six connections, will tell others that you are serious and competent about networking, new technology, and your career.

LinkedIn Limitations

From my experience, the biggest problem with LinkedIn is not the technology, but the expectation people have that it will do great things for their networking efforts. While there is a misunderstanding of what LinkedIn is, and how to get the best out of it, LinkedIn itself is quite clear about its offerings.

LinkedIn does not claim to compete in the "social networking space" like MySpace does. It has a different demographic than Facebook. Most people come into LinkedIn with certain expectations and probably the hope that it is going to be their networking mecca. In fact, it's not a

---

8. http://tinyurl.com/649qvw
blog.linkedin.com/2008/07/08/announcing-the-3/

networking mecca, rather it's a tool. For some people it is an extremely powerful tool; for others it is useless. It really comes down to understanding what the tool is. Here are some of LinkedIn's boundaries:

1. **LinkedIn is not a full-fledged social environment.** LinkedIn does not have the kinds of social interaction features that you'll find in places like Facebook where contacts have rich communication with one another. In fact, aside from InMail and Answers, there isn't much interaction at all. However, I think this is appropriate. Professionals don't limit their relationship-building to what they can do on a screen. Many professionals who network probably spend more time face-to-face or on the phone, rather than on social networks, to develop relationships. In other words, developing relationships can, and should, go offline. But some people still want LinkedIn to act like Facebook (which, in my opinion will only clutter the interface and confuse the user experience). I find this trivia rather interesting: LinkedIn launched May 5, 2003 (they are big fans of Cinco de Mayo), MySpace launched August 03, and Facebook launched February 2004 (these dates were pulled from Wikipedia).

2. **LinkedIn does not represent your entire network.** Some people think their entire network is found in LinkedIn. In reality, your entire network can't be in LinkedIn, unless you never go out and never talk on the phone. Are your plumber and your mechanic connected to you on LinkedIn? Mine aren't. Is everyone from your family reunion on LinkedIn, connected to you? I didn't think so.

3. **LinkedIn does not give you complete control of your relationships.** You can only connect to me if:

   a. I'm in LinkedIn and

   b. I agree to be your connection.

   This means you can't put every single person you meet into your LinkedIn network. Also, if I want to disconnect from you, I can do it with just a few clicks. This means you don't have any control over whether I stay in your network or not.

4. **LinkedIn does not allow you to control or change any information on your contacts.** As mentioned, people commonly confuse LinkedIn as a relationship management, or CRM (Customer Relationship Management), tool. These are software tools common to salespeople who use them to keep track of clients, pros-

pects and other contacts. Some of the most common CRM tools include Salesforce.com, GoldMine® and ACT! There are hundreds of CRM tools available.

5. **LinkedIn does not allow you to store relationship information about your contacts.** Building on the CRM idea, there's another level of information that you would want to keep track of. Imagine you and I had lunch this week—this is something that you might want to record somewhere (what we talked about, who paid, follow-up notes, etc.). You might want to create an action item, such as "Call Jason next Thursday to see if he talked to the VP of finance for me." Whether I'm going to talk to the VP of finance to plug you as a prospective employee or vendor, it is an important action item to follow up on! LinkedIn doesn't allow you to log meetings or thoughts, create action items, or even rank the relationship you have with me.

NOTE: in August 2008 LinkedIn introduced a section where I could store more details on each contact, but it's too early to know where that feature is headed. So you *can* put in notes for a contact, but not log entries or action items, and there doesn't appear to be a page to view these notes

---

6. **LinkedIn doesn't really provide much privacy.** If you are looking for privacy, stay away from the Internet! Your LinkedIn Profile will be available for people to see, no matter what you declare as "public" information. Your network will be available for others to see, at least implicitly, whether you allow your connections to browse your network or not. People can still find Profiles of your network contacts (see the Account & Settings chapter). I don't see this as a big deal, although I know some people still believe there is some kind of privacy in this world we live in. If this concerns you, LinkedIn might not be for you (but privacy issues on LinkedIn should really be the least of your privacy concerns).

7. **LinkedIn has a closed-communication system.** I don't like it when a service requires me to log in to its website in order to get information, or communicate with someone who is reaching out to me. InMail messages need to be replied to from within the InMail system. This protocol is common for Web services such as Facebook and Twitter (Twitter gives you the actual message via email but you can't reply back—the sending message is from a "do not reply" Twitter email address. I dislike this method because

I feel like it disrespects my time.) At least InMails show me the actual message in my email box so I don't need to login just to see what the message says.

I should note, after listing these limitations, I am not alone in thinking that LinkedIn **should not** resolve all (or any) of these things! While it would be cool to have a super-system, a silver-bullet to solve all of my networking needs, I do not advocate LinkedIn as the total solution. Here's why:

First, LinkedIn still needs to polish and fine-tune its core functionality. As a software developer I understand the danger of creating more features while the core is either not complete or not architected to work with so many peripheral features. You may have used software that introduces cool bells and whistles that aren't relevant to you, while you still have complaints about the core functionality. It's always appealing to develop a broader offering but it's usually not good for the end-users until you are ready to manage the growth.

Second, aside from spreading itself too thin technically, it can be an enormous distraction to design, support and maintain various additions to the core function. Designers need to make sure they do not break anything that exists (or should exist) in the core. The support team will need to learn new tools, philosophies and rules. Introducing any new feature outside of the core can add exponential complexity with regard to maintaining the software and hardware. It's not to say that LinkedIn can't tackle any new non-core features, but there is a reason why companies in every industry stay within their core competency and outsource the rest.

Third, there is a new trend in software development, especially web-based applications, where you develop the very best program to accomplish ABC and then find a complementary web-based application to accomplish XYZ. This way, multiple companies share the burdens of designing, staying relevant, maintaining, etc. LinkedIn should be the very best application to find and be found, and to portray your professional image (to a degree). It should find other systems that make up for its shortcomings, and partner with them. Right now this is called "mashups" and there are thousands of examples. Here are a few:

- TypePad® blogs mashing up with CAPTCHA technology. If you leave a comment on a TypePad® blog you'll likely have to type in the letters/numbers from an image—the technology is sometimes supplied by CAPTCHA.

- Google Maps integrations with sites to find sex offenders, bars, transit lines or hundreds of other useful things. GoogleMapsMania[9] is a website with information on the Google Maps mashups.

- LinkedIn provides a common example—that of integrating job board functionality into an existing site. LinkedIn is not a job board but it looks like they have job board functionality. In fact, they do, part of which is done in-house and part of which is provided by a mashup partner, Simply Hired.

- JibberJobber.com has mashups with Google Maps to see your networks on a map, Skype to call them with one click, Anagram™[10] to quickly capture email signatures and add them to your network, and indeed to search multiple job boards.

I can see the day when LinkedIn tries to attack each of these issues and begins to become the silver bullet application for networking. It will always have stiff competition from various angles, and won't be able to provide a better CRM tool than Salesforce.com, or a better social environment than Facebook, but it can be the very best at what it does. We'll see where they decide to go strategically, which will have a significant impact on the list of strengths and weaknesses. For now they are good at what they do, and the limitations should not be a hindrance to actively using the tool.

LinkedIn made an interesting announcement in June 2007 regarding APIs, which will allow programmers to develop programs and interfaces to LinkedIn. This is very similar to the mashups idea (which depends on APIs) but can be more powerful. In the first edition of this book I wrote "it will be interesting to see how the development of APIs rolls out, and what kinds of complementary tools are developed." Since then I've seen a few API/mashup things, but not much. LinkedIn has estab-

---

9. http://googlemapsmania.blogspot.com
10. http://getanagram.com

lished strategic relationships with BusinessWeek,[11] CNBC and others, and some sites have been able to use the APIs to incorporate some LinkedIn functionality into their stuff (JibberJobber has a few places where we mashup with LinkedIn). Unfortunately, we're not seeing much else from LinkedIn as far as interfacing with other systems, and I'm guessing they are going to restrict access to a handful of strategic partners. I hope I'm proven wrong.

Chapter Summary

*   LinkedIn is a powerful tool, not a silver bullet.

*   LinkedIn should be a part of your networking strategy, complemented with other tools and techniques.

*   Different people use LinkedIn for different reasons—why do you use it?

---

11. http://tinyurl.com/yrzwqn
blog.linkedin.com/2008/03/27/get-your-inside-connections-with-business-week-simplyhired/

"I'm a huge fan, user and promoter of LinkedIn. I've used it to network into the technology field from print advertising and get my current job in a new high-growth department. Currently a friend and I are founding an online apparel business. I've used LinkedIn to find manufacturers, screen-printers, and as a resource for investors to research our management team."
-- **Jimmy Hendricks,** *http://www.CollarFree.com*

"So far I primarily see my involvement on LinkedIn similar to having money in a savings account. It's not something I often tap, but something that's reassuring to have available when the need arises. I've also used LinkedIn as a journalist to make contact with people who might have expert knowledge on a topic."
-- **Bernie Wagenblast, Editor of the Transportation Communications Newsletter**

"My favorite thing about LinkedIn is finding old contacts. I discovered an old college friend and several coworkers who moved on to other companies. It was nice to read about what they'd been up to in their Profiles and reconnect."
-- **Pete Johnson, HP.com Chief Architect**

"It's not about 'collecting and trading your friends' as I originally saw LinkedIn. It's really about visibility into relationships that you wouldn't know existed otherwise. Help others use the tool better. The more people who know how to use the tool effectively, the more effective it is for everyone. What a terrific way to take your relationship to the next level!"
-- **Scott Ingram,** *http://www.NetworkinAustin.com*

Chapter 2: What is LinkedIn?

3 Your Profile

This chapter talks about optimizing your Profile. Two reasons to have a well-done Profile are:

1. to increase your chances of being found, and
2. to effectively communicate information about you.

While you shouldn't write a novel about your professional life, you can construct your Profile in a way that conveys your professional brand, including your strengths, knowledge, experience, and other things that help me understand the value you bring to me. Here are some things to think about with your Profile:

1. How will old friends find you? Make sure you put names of schools, companies, clubs etc. in your Profile.
2. How will recruiters, hiring managers or potential business partners find you? Again, make sure you put names of schools, companies and clubs, as recruiters look for candidates with specific experience, affiliations or work history. Include any keywords and jargon that you would put on a resume so a recruiter looking for a "PHP programmer

with CSS and Adobe skills" or a "Project manager with a PMP" can be found. Many recruiters have had training on how to search on LinkedIn and use various search techniques to find exactly what they are looking for.

3. What will the first impression be? You should spend at least as much time on a LinkedIn Profile as you would on a resume. Whether you are looking for a job or not, you never know who is looking for you. Ensure you leave a sharp first impression by having proper grammar, spelling and composition of the text in your Profile.

Here are some considerations:

People look for potential connections based on things you have in common, like where you went to school. For example, let's say you went to college at UCLA. You might have a classmate who has been looking for you but can't remember your name...when he looks for other UCLA alumni he might recognize your name.

Once when I was looking at my LinkedIn home page I clicked on the "Reconnect with past Colleagues" link (scroll to the bottom of the home page and you should see contacts from previous employers), and then clicked on a company that I worked at over seven years earlier. One of my key contacts at that company had gone on to a different company but, because he had put the company name in his Profile, I was able to find him and we've since reconnected! This is one of the more powerful features of LinkedIn but it relies on people filling out their Profile with sufficient information.

When creating your Profile make sure you fill out as much as you can, with as much detail as you can. Again, this is not a time to write a novel. If you think about the conciseness of a resume and the tactics of search engine logic you should be able to come up with a great Profile. What exactly does this mean?

When you create a resume you have various sections, such as a summary, job history, education, etc. LinkedIn has similar sections with a few differences. These differences aren't significant and it's safe to consider a well-done LinkedIn Profile to be similar to a well-done resume. Here are a few differences:

1. Most LinkedIn Profiles do not have bulleted formatting with quantifying proof of how valuable you were to a particular company. For example, on your resume you might put bullet after bullet of statements like "increased department revenues by 150% and profits by 250% in 18 months." You can include that in a LinkedIn Profile but you usually find the description of Profiles to be more narrative, rather than highlighted bullet-points. You can put in hyphens, asterisks or some other bullet character to create a list, but it's not quite the same as real bullets.

2. LinkedIn has a section at the bottom of each Profile to declare your interests, with predefined interests such as career opportunities, job inquiries, getting back in touch, and a few others. This helps people who view your Profile know whether you are approachable for certain things or not. Some people will respect your list of interests while others may still attempt to contact you for something even though you do not list it. (Not everyone who is interested in career opportunities is going to declare that there, especially if their current employer doesn't know they are interested in other opportunities!)

3. If you are a member of any LinkedIn Groups, the Groups will show up on your Profile (unless you choose to not show the Group image). You can learn more about this in the LinkedIn Groups chapter.

Aside from a Profile that reads well, consider how the LinkedIn search engine will find (or miss!) your Profile. Keep in mind the public Profile is also indexed by search engines such as Yahoo! and Google™, and the advice in this section applies to those search engines also.

There are basic principles behind "search engine optimization" (SEO). With SEO you are trying to optimize a page (or Profile) so search engines bring it up first (or, in the first batch of results). Optimize your Profile with SEO in mind. Here are some tricks you can incorporate as you develop your Profile:

1. School names - include the full name (University of Virginia) as well as the common abbreviation (UVA).

2. Company names - just as you did with the school names, make sure you put the official and common names of the companies where you worked. If your company is a subsidiary of a larger company, put the name of the larger company also. That way if a recruiter is looking for someone from either the main company or the subsidiary, they are more likely to come across your Profile.

3. Technical skills - just as a recruiter looks for "project managers" or someone who is a "project manager professional" they might search for "PMP" (Project Management Professional), or someone who is a member of the "PMI" (Project Management Institute). You increase your odds of being found if you list each version (abbreviated and spelled out) of each company or school somewhere within your LinkedIn Profile.

Aside from writing your Profile so the search engine finds you, consider writing it so the person reading your Profile is impressed by the value you bring to a relationship. Deb Dib, The CEO Coach, wrote a powerful article for CEOs titled **LinkedIn—What It Is and Why You Need to Be On It**.[12] Check out the eight Profiles she links to, which are all examples of excellent LinkedIn Profiles, whether you are a CxO or not!

TIP: Lonny Gulden, a recruiter in Minnesota, suggests including company names from any company you worked with but changed their name (merger, acquisition, etc.) Recruiters might look for ex-employees of those defunct companies.

---

12. http://tinyurl.com/59jtvd
job-hunt.org/executive-job-search/linkedin-for-executives.shtml

Perhaps one of the best resources for optimizing your Profile so it appeals to people *and* LinkedIn's search algorithm is Guy Kawasaki's famous LinkedIn Profile Extreme Makeover (you can find it by typing "Kawasaki & LinkedIn" into a search engine, or going to http://blog.guykawasaki.com/2007/01/linkedin_profil.html). Apparently Guy has one of the most viewed Profiles on LinkedIn and he got special help from LinkedIn to make his Profile better!

The advice from LinkedIn is to flesh out each section of the Profile and put in more details. Some of the recommendations include:

- "Write Recommendations" - this is a way to get YOUR NAME, with a link back to your LinkedIn Profile, on someone else's Profile.

- "Ask a question, answer questions" - again, a way to get a link to your Profile on a totally different section of LinkedIn.

- "Get a vanity URL" - this is easy and free. Simply go into the "edit Profile" screen to do it—basically your URL could go from something like "http://linkedin.com/pub/1/234/1344" to "http://linkedin.com/in/jasonalba."

- In the Summary section, "Add substance...this is your 'elevator pitch.'"

And on and on. This is solid advice. Once you flesh out your Profile, you rarely have to revisit it to keep it up to date. Of course, you should keep it updated as things change. Scott Allen shares a story on his blog[13] of how a timely Profile update ended up being a $5,000 decision.

Your Public Profile is what people see if they are not logged into LinkedIn. It's important that you think about what to show and what to hide. Click on Account & Settings and then My Public Profile, where you can choose what you show and hide, all managed through this screen:

---

13. http://tinyurl.com/365p3c
linkedintelligence.com/the-5000-profile-update/

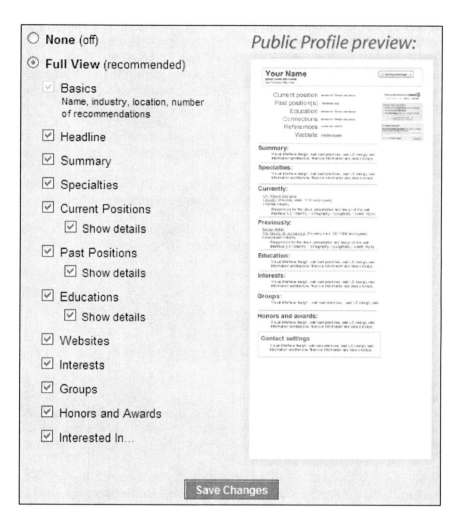

Figure 1: Public Profile Preview

All of the optional things to show or hide in your Public Profile are things you should have in your Profile already. Don't worry about creating two Profiles (which is against the User Agreement); You are simply designating what information people can see if they are not logged in. I have two thoughts regarding this feature:

First, you need to provide as much information as you can so visitors who come across your Profile can get the gist of who you are without having to login (or worse, create a new account and then login).

Second, consider your personal comfort level regarding privacy. If you are comfortable putting up certain information on your regular, non-Public Profile, which is available to over twenty-eight million people, why not let non-LinkedIn people see it?

I've heard people express concerns about privacy with their LinkedIn Profile. The purpose of a Profile is not to record private data—it is to showcase who you are in a professional setting. It's great to be concerned about privacy, but with the technology available today there are dozens of places someone can go to find your personal information, including your contact information, professional history, even your social security number!

Having a complete Profile is your opportunity to express what you want expressed and not just leave it up to the search engines to portray who you are. The Profile is central to your experience on LinkedIn, so make sure you spend time getting it right.

Chapter Summary

- Set up your Profile as completely as possible so that others can find you.

- Make sure you check spelling, grammar and overall readability of your Profile.

- Take advantage of things such as the vanity URL and Recommendations to make your Profile look more professional.

- Allow others to see a lot of information on your Public Profile.

"I'm starting to think LinkedIn may be Resume 2.0, but I'm not 100% convinced yet. When I beefed up my Profile, I actually copied and pasted bullet points from my latest conventional resume and now that thing is searchable for all the world to see. That's a lot different than posting it in some random place on a few job sites. It's in a neutral place where you expect pressure-reduced interactions with others."
-- Pete Johnson, HP.com Chief Architect

"You only get 3 links, so use them wisely—I would encourage you to use the links for your blog, a full page of other endorsements about you, and your portfolio or book or something else that shows your expertise."
-- Phil Gerbyshak, *http://www.MakeItGreatGuy.com*

"When you set up your Profile, make sure it's a snapshot—no one wants to read a detailed autobiography. And don't forget to proofread!"
-- Christine Dennison, *http://www.TheJobSearchCoach.com*

"Your LinkedIn Profile is a critical part of your online identity. Make sure to complete it with information that conveys what you do, the value you deliver, and the audience you serve; in other words, have it reflect your personal brand."
-- Walter Akana, *http://www.Threshold-Consulting.com*

"I think the Status Update feature is one of the coolest things on the LinkedIn profile! Used strategically and well, the Status Update line can be used to promote your business, products and personal brand to your network. I use it to promote my blog posts, speaking engagements and networking events or conferences I'm attending to facilitate the possiblity of connecting in person or on the web with those in my network. As a Recruiter, I also use the Status Update to make my network aware of opportunities that I'm recruiting for. I have a fairly large network—over 1,500 connections —so that's 1,500+ opportunities to reach candidates or get referrals—and it works! I also encourage job seekers to use the Status Update feature to make sure their network knows that they are currently searching for a new opportunity. Regularly updating your Status keeps you on "top of mind" and on the Home page of those in your network."

-- Jennifer McClure, Executive Recruiter/Executive Coach, http://www.cincyrecruiter.com

4 Account & Settings

There is an Account & Settings link at the top right of every page that takes you to one of the most important menus in LinkedIn. It's critical to understand what's here so you can customize your user experience. The account section shows you what you get at your current account level and allows you to see what you could get if you upgrade.

My account shows that I have 4 of 5 Introductions left and no InMails, and notifies me that if I wanted more access or privileges I can upgrade. I personally don't need to upgrade although I know many people have upgraded as they are in a more active mode of networking, whether they are looking for talent, jobs or business partners.

Upgrading is simple. Right now there are four different types of accounts in a comparison chart. The chart shows comparisons between Business, Business Plus and Pro and shows features such as the number of InMails you can send and receive, enhanced ability to communicate with others in LinkedIn, access to the "OpenLink Network," the ability to get sneak peeks on new features and even priority customer service.

Personal	Business	Business plus	Pro
Free	$19.95 per month or $199.50 per year (2 months free)	$50 per month or $500 per year (2 months free)	$200 per month or $2000 per year (2 months free)
	⇨ Upgrade	⇨ Upgrade	⇨ Upgrade

Figure 2: Account Types

Last year there was a special level for $6.95/month, but that has been discontinued (I understand those who had it can still have it, but they don't offer it anymore). Unless you have a very specific reason to build a huge network through LinkedIn (if you are a recruiter, or have some other business need), a free Personal account should be just fine. If you find you are too limited, then check out the differences between various upgrade plans and choose the one that's best for you.

Settings is one of the most important places to visit if you feel like you get too much or too little correspondence (emails) from LinkedIn. There are various parts of LinkedIn that want to communicate with you. For example, if someone wants to get in touch with you, LinkedIn will let you know. If someone asks a question in Answers, and you are in their network, LinkedIn will let you know (depending on how they asked the question).

The default settings may not meet your needs. I found I was getting more emails than I wanted from LinkedIn. At the same time, some of my contacts weren't getting questions I submitted to Answers (they had changed their Settings so they only received Questions via email). Frustrated by too many emails, I finally went to the Settings section and set up my account so I got only what I wanted and filtered the rest out. I wasn't limiting my ability to see information; I was just choosing whether I wanted to get certain notices via email or in my mailbox in LinkedIn.

Figure 3: Message Settings

Here's how I have my Settings:

- **Introductions and InMails** - I chose to accept these via email so if someone tries to get in touch with me I won't miss it (the landing page is too cluttered for me to read every single thing, and since I don't login every day I knew I would miss something).

- **Invitations** - I want an invitation email immediately. Someone is reaching out to me and I want to be able to react as soon as possible (strike while the iron is hot).

- **Profile Updates** - I like to know what's changed in my network and appreciate the email I get (no more than once a week) telling me who has changed their job title or otherwise updated their Profile. I also set my own Profile so that if I change something my contacts will get an email (if, of course, they have their Setting to receive emails for these types of notices).

- **Job Notifications** - These are notices that come from people in my network. I am not in an active job search and have found the job notifications I get are irrelevant to me (or others in my network). Therefore, I've chosen to turn off the emails and only see job notifications on my home page when I login. I usually archive them right away.

- **Recommendation Notifications** - I don't want to get an email notification when one of my contacts recommends a service provider (I'd rather just read it on the website). Part of this is because my network is kind of big (it's not huge by any measure). If you have a network with people you know and trust, seeing who they recommend could be valuable.

- **Answers Notifications** - I choose to view new questions from my network on the website, as opposed to by email. Part of my regular LinkedIn maintenance is to enter the Answers section to see what I might be able to answer. If someone answers a question I asked, I immediately get an email for each answer.

- **Email Tips** - You can choose to receive emails from the LinkedIn team with "useful tips." I have this set to receive them (they say they "will never send you more than one email a month"), although I don't remember getting any of these emails yet (it's been over two years). I find it harmless, since it would only be sent once a month and I really am interested in what they would highlight.

Another Setting you should know about is the "Connections Browse," under **Privacy Settings**. I find this to be one of the most interesting (and controversial) options in the Settings area. On the one hand, it seems to be totally contradictory to what I think LinkedIn is all about (the ability to see who is in my contact's network). On the other hand, this option somewhat respects the privacy of my network contacts and people in their network. You need to understand that no matter what this Setting is, your contacts can still see who you are connected to!

The default setting allows all of your first degree contacts to see all of your other first degree connections. Even if you choose to not allow your contacts to see your network, I can still find your contacts through a search. For example, let's say you have someone in your network who is a project manager in Seattle. When I search for "project manager" or "Seattle" I will find everyone in my first three degrees (including your first and second degree contacts), **even if** you have said I can't browse your network. Notice the difference between "browse" and "see"—browsing is showing me a nicely-formatted page with everyone in your network. Seeing is the ability to actually find the contact and read their Profile. You cannot block me from seeing people in your network, I just have to know what to search for to find them.

Make sure you have the right email addresses associated with your account. I have two email addresses that I check regularly (one for the business I own and another through Gmail). Since I easily send out fifty emails a day, some from my business account and others from my Gmail account, I made sure people who want to invite me could use either address. Why? Some of my contacts only know me from the Gmail account while others know me from my business account. Fortunately, LinkedIn allows my contacts to send me an invitation to either address.

Figure 4: Email Accounts

Make sure the primary email address is one you own and use! I once saw an email thread where the discussion was based around a person developing a LinkedIn network while working at their job and the employer claiming the network belonged to the company. This is an interesting claim, but I can see the employer actually keeping the network. To avoid this potential conflict, make sure the email addresses on your account are solely controlled by you. You can get free email accounts from Hotmail, Yahoo!, Gmail and a host of other services. My second email address is a company address, but I consider this a small exception since I own the company!

Here's a summary of my Settings:

Setting Name	How I've Set My Account
Introductions and InMails	Twice a week, via email
Invitations	Email me immediately
Profile Updates	Once a week (if there are any), via email

Setting Name	How I've Set My Account
Job Notifications	No email; I'll look on the website
Recommendation Notifications	No email; I'll look on the website
Answers Notifications–new questions	No email; I'll look on the website
Answers Notifications–someone answers my question	Email me immediately
Email Tips	Email me monthly
Connections Browse	Allow others to browse my connections
Email Addresses	My Gmail account is the primary address, my JibberJobber account is a secondary address

Chapter Summary

- Dive into the Account & Settings pages to set up your preferences—this will determine when you receive emails and when you don't!

- If you have multiple email addresses make sure you put them in your account—that way others can connect with you by sending an invitation to either email account.

- Turning off the Network Browse can preclude your first degree contacts from seeing the complete list of all of your other first degree contacts, but does not block those contacts from showing up in search results.

"Learn the site. There is a lot of useful help listed under Help & FAQ. If you take the time to review your Account & Settings and set your account up properly, your time on LinkedIn will be much easier."
-- Sheilah Etheridge, owner of SME Management

5 Connecting with Others

At the center of your LinkedIn experience is how and when to connect with other people. Consider a spectrum where one end represents people who are open networkers and accept any invitation they get (and, who freely extend invitations to anyone they can). The other end of the spectrum represents people who are more conservative about who they connect with.

Figure 5: Open/Closed Networker Spectrum

There are issues surrounding the open/closed spectrum concept. I'll explain characteristics of both ends of the spectrum, noting there are legitimate reasons for any position (open, closed or in-between), and you need to decide what your own connection policy should be.

Open Networking

There is an acronym that you will likely encounter in your LinkedIn experience: LION. LION stands for "LinkedIn Open Networker." I wrote a blog post titled I'm a LION—Hear Me ROAR[14] that got a number of comments, and stirred a debate on MyVirtualPowerForum. There are a lot of ideas on being a LION, and the comments in that post really paint a broad picture of this issue.This refers to a person interested in having as many connections as they can get and indicates a general willingness to accept an invitation from anyone. Open networkers tend to subscribe to the theory that having more connections means you have more channels to reach a key person. You can see a list of LIONS at http://MyLink500.com.

Arguments for being a LION are based around having a large number of contacts and being able to search on or otherwise interact with, those contacts. For example, if you are a recruiter you want to have access to "passive candidates," which refers to potential hires who are not active job seekers. If you have 100 connections in LinkedIn it's possible to search for a specific candidate and find someone. But if you have 4,000 first degree connections you have a much higher probability of finding the passive candidates who match your needs! This is why many recruiters on LinkedIn are "open networkers."

While I use recruiters as an example, there are others who find open networking beneficial. These people are typically in roles where they actively look for people for one reason or another. This might include salespeople, business people, entrepreneurs, or other power connectors (a phrase coined by Keith Ferrazzi to describe people who are in a profession which facilitates making lots of connections).

---

14. http://tinyurl.com/linkedin-LION
imonlinkedinnowwhat.com/2008/07/31/im-a-lion-hear-me-roar/

Figure 6: Import Contacts

Open networkers can quickly and easily grow their personal LinkedIn networks by downloading the Outlook toolbar and inviting all of their Outlook connections to join LinkedIn. In addition you can import your contact lists from online email accounts, including Yahoo!, AOL, Hotmail, and Gmail.

Beware that everyone has a limit on the number of connection *invitations*! The current limit is 3,000. It may seem like a lot, but consider many LIONs have more than 3,000 connections and are always looking for more! If you reach 3,000 connections you can request more from LinkedIn customer service. Additional invitations are usually granted in blocks of 100.

Sending out a lot of connection invitations, especially to people who don't know you very well, may get your account suspended. There is a mechanism within LinkedIn that allows others to flag you, as they can click a button on the invitation that says "I don't know (your name)." If you get five people who click this button, you will lose some invitation privileges. Right now you get a red warning box that says you have received five "I don't know" clicks, and you have to have the email address of anyone you invite until you email customer support and clear things up.

It's wise to prepare your contacts, outside of LinkedIn, before you invite them through LinkedIn. If you end up suspended, contact LinkedIn customer service to get it resolved. Usually they ask you to agree to their Terms of Service, and then reinstate your account.

TIP: To avoid getting penalized, send an email to a potential contact first, asking if they are willing to connect on LinkedIn. If they say yes, send the invitation through LinkedIn.

There has been confusion amongst LinkedIn users about whether LinkedIn encourages you to be an open networker (based on the tools they provide and the ease of inviting a lot of people) or to be a closed networker (based on the discipline they enforce if you invite too many people who don't know you or are inclined to flag you). You'll fall somewhere between, and need to choose a connections strategy that makes sense for your own situation.

Closed Networking

Closed networkers, or perhaps "conservative networkers," are on the other end of the Open/Closed Networker Spectrum. Closed networkers are those who only connect with those they "know and trust." Instead of accepting every single connection request they ever get, they'll evaluate the relationship with the person requesting the connection and only connect when they feel comfortable connecting.

Many people who are conservative networkers on LinkedIn are "open networkers" in a more general sense. Many will have more relaxed standards on other social networking sites, or face-to-face networking, regarding who they connect with or talk to. For them, it's not so much an indication of their overall networking philosophy as it is a decision about how to use LinkedIn based on its design and purpose, and their needs.

There are three things a conservative networker can do, in response to a connection request from someone they aren't ready to connect with:

1. **Ignore the request.** In LinkedIn, the best way to do this is to click "Archive," so it doesn't sit in your inbox.
2. **IDK.** Click the "I don't know this person" button which adds one more vote similar to "mark this person as a spammer" and potentially get the inviter's account penalized.
3. **Wait until you get more information about the inviter.** You can let it sit in your box while you try and figure out who the inviter is, and why you should connect. This approach takes extra time and effort, while the first two are quick resolutions and easy to do.

Figure 7: Responses to a Connection Request

If you want to connect with a closed networker, I recommend establishing a relationship with them outside of LinkedIn until you can ask them "would you like to connect on LinkedIn?" This way, when you send them the invitation, they are expecting it and are more likely to accept it (unless they have a lapse in memory).

There is a preference in LinkedIn under "Connections Browse" that says: "Allow your connections to view the rest of your connections list?" The default is set to "yes." If you change this to "no," then no one can browse your connections. Your contacts can still find out who your connections are when they do a search (because your first degree contacts are their second degree contacts, which show up in their search results), so you can't hide your connections. For more information on this see the Account & Settings chapter.

The Canned Invitation

Here's another topic that gets a lot of attention—is there a cheesier way to invite someone to LinkedIn than using the default invitation that LinkedIn provides? When you invite someone to LinkedIn there is a default invitation you can change, but you have to remember to change it—and it's easy to miss! Right now the default invitation is:

"I'd like to add you to my professional network on LinkedIn."

Almost every blog post I've read regarding the default invitation is negative, and many folks recommend you make it more personal. I totally agree! Leaving the invitation text as the canned text is the same as saying "I don't care about you—you are just a number to me."

When I invite someone to connect in LinkedIn I change the default invitation so the recipient knows I am serious about a relationship. I definitely recommend you incorporate your style in the invitations you send through LinkedIn.

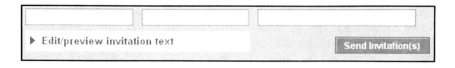

Figure 8: Edit Invitation

Scott Allen has a tongue-in-cheek blog post[15] on various different types of invitations that are quite fun, with different creative approaches. The best invitations I receive are concise and include the following information (in any order):

- **Here's who I am.** Not bragging, or listing all of your wonderful skills and experiences, but let me know something about you (without making me go look at your Profile).

---

15. http://tinyurl.com/3c98wm
linkedintelligence.com/better-boilerplates/

Chapter 5: Connecting with Others

- **Here's how I came across your Profile.** Did you find me in a LinkedIn search? Did you meet me at a networking event, or find me on a Yahoo! Group? Let me know how you found me, so I can put our relationship into perspective.

- **Here's why I'd like to connect.** This is the value proposition. You don't HAVE TO have a reason to connect, other than just wanting to connect and get to know one another better. Every relationship starts somewhere. But if you have a more specific reason to connect, let me know what it is.

Your Connection Strategy

Regardless of where you fall on the Open/Closed Spectrum, consider whom you connect with. In The Virtual Handshake the authors talk about ensuring you have diversity in your network. Think about what that means—if you are an accountant, connected only with other accountants, you don't have diversity. Who are the professionals an accountant works with? CFOs, CEOs, accounting vendors, tax professionals, HR professionals, IT professionals, and more. See the diversity the accountant could have in her network?

In addition to ensuring diversity with other professions, think about diversity in industries. What contacts could you easily connect with from complementary industries? Think about your industry, and who serves you—who are your vendors and service providers? Think about who they work with; other clients, maybe in other industries. Also, who are your clients? They might also be in other industries. As you include these people in your LinkedIn network, your diversity will grow in your first degree network, and you'll see a remarkable difference in your second and third degrees.

Finally, think about where your connections are. Do you do business locally? You should have a significant amount of local contacts. Do you do a lot of business in Seattle, or Florida? Grow your networks where your clients and prospects are.

Final Thoughts Regarding Connections

Issues surrounding invitations and connections are well debated on email forums and blogs. Some people are offended by those who don't share their views on how to use LinkedIn to network, and others pass judgment on those who have a different style (even though their objectives may be different). You need to figure out what is best for you and use the tool the right way—for you. Being aware of how others use LinkedIn and where they lie on the open/closed spectrum will help you understand why they may accept or reject a connection invitation, or even how they react to Introduction requests. One of the most frequent questions I get is, "if I disconnect from someone, will they get a notice?" No one gets a notice when you disconnect from them—so feel free to clean up your network as often as you wish.

Chapter Summary

* There are pros and cons to open and closed networking strategies—you need to determine what's best for you.

* Beware of abusing connection invitations, which might get your account penalized.

* When you invite someone to connect, be sensitive to the invitation message and customize it when appropriate.

"LinkedIn works best when you use it with focused outcomes in mind. I am always open to invitations, but take a look at my Profile first and tell me why you are interested in connecting with me. A little 'wooing' goes a long way!"
-- Garland Coulson, http://www.FreeTrafficBar.com

"I asked people to join my network due to their 'status'...what a mistake. Invite only people you trust, regardless of their position or status."
-- David Armstrong, http://www.BounceBase.com

"Most of my LinkedIn contacts come through an electronic newsletter I edit that's focused on the transportation industry. I sent an invitation to the subscribers who were already part of LinkedIn to connect with me. I see it as one more way readers of the newsletter might gain value from being subscribers. Since the subscriber list is private, those who are part of my LinkedIn network can see others who are part of my network and make a connection, either directly or through me."
-- Bernie Wagenblast, Editor of the Transportation Communications Newsletter

"I wasted several InMails and Introductions when I could have simply hit the 'Add [contact name] to your Network' button because I thought I had to know their current emails to use that. I think this is very common."
-- Ingo Dean, Senior Manager of Global IT at Virage Logic

"Be open to a diverse network. You never know who you can help or who can help you. It's ok if you only want known people in your network or only people from one industry etc. But the more diverse your network is the more rewarding it can be. This is especially true if you want to gain business from the site. People in your industry most likely won't need your services, but those in other industries may."
-- Sheilah Etheridge, owner of SME Management

> "Links to people can be broken—if you connected to a person that is suddenly sending you a boatload of spam just because you're 'LinkedIn buddies,' you can (and should) break the link."
>
> **-- Phil Gerbyshak,** _http://www.MakeItGreatGuy.com_

> "I hate receiving a LinkedIn 'invitation to connect' template. They lack authenticity and make me feel the person does not value the relationship enough to compose a personalized message. Take the time to create a touch point with your contact...it is well worth the extra effort."
>
> **-- Barbara Safani,** _http://www.CareerSolvers.com_

Part II
Making it Work for You

Now that you have your Profile and account setup, let's get into the meat of LinkedIn. In Part II we'll talk about what it means to connect with other LinkedIn users, how to search for people, what Degrees of Separation is, how to give and accept Recommendations, how to use the Jobs and Services section, how LinkedIn Groups could benefit you and what you should be doing with LinkedIn Answers.

6 Searching

Searching on LinkedIn was my first great frustration. I had fewer than five people in my network when I searched for management jobs in Utah. I was totally surprised to see no results on this simple search! This chapter talks about having a better search experience than I had. Here's what I've learned since those days of five connections:

Increase the size of your network. If you are interested in people and opportunities in your city, look for more local connections. If you are interested in people and opportunities in your industry or profession, expand your LinkedIn network with industry and professional contacts. As your network grows with the right kinds of connections, you are more likely to get relevant search results. Your search results are based on your connections.

Connect with a few super-connectors. Super-connectors are LinkedIn users who have a lot of connections—hundreds, or thousands of connections. Connecting with super-connectors increases your visibility in the system significantly. They enhance your ability to find and to be found. You don't have to connect with very many super-connectors, as they seem to be connected with one another. Connecting with even two or three could give you visibility into about 20–25% of the entire LinkedIn network. As you connect with the super-connectors, try to get to know them and be more than just another of their several thousand links.

Use the basic search form found on every page when you are logged in. This form allows you to search for People, Jobs, Answers, your inbox, and Groups, using whatever keywords you want:

Figure 9: LinkedIn Basic Search

Understand advanced search options. Usually the quick search allows you to find what you're looking for. However, there are times when you'll want to get more specific results based on certain criteria. Scott Allen talks about using LinkedIn to plan a business trip, specifically to fill up your spare time. Scott suggests you do a special search using the advanced form to search for people in the city where you will be, like this:

Figure 10: LinkedIn Special Search

You can only choose the country and ZIP code filter if you are in certain countries (including the United States, Canada and United Kingdom). If you are an international traveller, you won't always be able to do this. For example, with fewer than 300 first degree contacts I did a search on "manager" in India and found at least 500 connections in my immediate network (that is, anyone who is one, two or three degrees away from me).

There are other useful features in the advanced search form, such as:

Keywords - This could be any keyword, perhaps a company name, a technology, the name of a certification, a club or school, etc. If you want to get results for a company name, you should put that name in the Company field.

Name - The LAST NAME of the person. This is clear in the "Name search" right above the "Advanced search" by noting "Last name required." The same is true in this box also. I did a search for "Jason" and found people with the last name of Jason but no hits of anyone with Jason as a first name.

Title - You can choose to limit the search to current titles only. Otherwise it will show Profiles of people who have *ever* held the title (as per their Profile). This can be very useful!

Company - Same as the Title, you can limit to current companies only, or search for current and past companies. Make sure to try various versions of a company name (i.e. GE and General Electric), subsidiaries, etc.

Location - You can choose the country (and zip code for certain countries). You can also say whether they are "in the location," "near the location" or "willing to travel" to that location. This feels kind of clunky—I did a search on "Mexico" and came up with over 500 hits just in my network. How am I supposed to know who to connect with if I'm going to Mexico City as opposed to Monterrey? It doesn't seem possible to get as specific as necessary if you are looking for contacts in many countries.

Industry - These are predefined industries people put on their own Profile and include things such as Research, Wine and Spirits, Machinery and Alternative Dispute Resolution! Because this list is not all-inclusive I recommend you *put industry information in your summary*, which can increase your chances of being found.

Interested In - This will narrow the search results to people who are interested in "consulting opportunities," "hiring managers," "potential employees," "deal-making contacts" and other such interests.

Joined Your Network - Allows you to filter your results based on when they joined your network and includes options such as "since your last login," "in the last 3 months" or even "any time."

Sort By - Allows you to show the order in which the results are sorted, with options such as "Degrees and Recommendations" and "number of connections." This should allow you to find something more relevant to what you are looking for as opposed to sifting through hundreds of hits.

The results you see are shown in two tabs: your first, second and third degree contacts are in the first tab while results from the entire LinkedIn database are in the second tab. The bigger your network, and the better connected they are, the better results you'll get in the first tab.

As I mentioned, searching was one of my frustrations with LinkedIn. If you can figure it out you will have a powerful tool to help you find some great contacts, whether you are traveling to a new city, looking for more industry contacts to network with, or looking for employees, partners, vendors, etc.

You can search the Internet for tips on optimizing LinkedIn, but if you are looking for the ultimate resource on LinkedIn searching I strongly recommend Shally Steckerl's Advanced LinkedIn Cheatsheet and Advanced LinkedIn Networking—two quick-reference documents with a lot of tips, tricks and hacks for LinkedIn power users. Fortunately LinkedIn allows you to do Boolean searches (using AND, OR and NOT), use quotes, inclusions, exclusions, etc. For example, try any of the following searches in the Advanced Search page (you can put these in the keywords or company or title fields):

- Google NOT Microsoft

- Google AND Microsoft

- php -programmer -linux -javascript -css -html -mysql (the + means it has to include the phrase, the - means the Profile cannot include the phrase)

- "project management institute"—for an exact match of the term

- "project management institute" AND (Microsoft OR SUN)

If you need more on advanced searching in LinkedIn, steal some tricks from Google's search tips page,[16] or check out Shally's LinkedIn Cheatsheets at the Job Machine website, or at the top of http://www.ImOnLinkedInNowWhat.com.

Chapter Summary

- The number of Profiles you can search on is tied to the size of your network.

- The advanced search form allows you to really narrow down your search, based on industry, job title, zip code and more.

- Use Boolean and advanced search techniques to narrow down the search results.

- Shally's Cheatsheet is an excellent resource to getting more out of LinkedIn. It is quite technical, but very powerful. You can find a link to purchase it at the top of ImOnLinkedInNowWhat.com.

---

16. http://tinyurl.com/3augdn
google.com/support/bin/static.py?page=search-guides.html&ctx=basics&hl=en

"Take the time to look through the networks of your direct connects. This is where you can easily find people you'd like to connect with and you'll know you can ask your contact to help with the connection."
-- Scott Ingram, http://www.NetworkinAustin.com

"Be sure to search on the actual leadership competencies that matter instead of keywords like job title and company name. Some of the best and most interesting thought leaders of the future I've met on LinkedIn are the ones who haven't worked at cookie cutter company X doing cookie cutter job Y. The team you assemble won't be filled with the limiting beliefs of your competitors from several years ago which is a major plus."
-- David Dalka, Senior Marketing and Business Development Professional, http://www.daviddalka.com

7 Understanding Degrees of Separation

The basic idea behind degrees of separation is that you are only so many degrees away from anyone (usually six). For example, if I wanted to meet the Prime Minister of some obscure country, I should be able to network into him or her and only have to go to my fifth degree connection before I get an introduction.

A few years ago there was a "six degrees from Kevin Bacon"[17] experiment, and recently network television has done similar experiments (without the celebrity). The degrees of separation measurement that LinkedIn uses gives you an interesting perspective on your network.

By looking at the number of contacts in your network, you can get a sense of the breadth (how wide) and depth (how deep) of your network. Consider your first degree connections as the width of your network, and anything below that as the depth of your network. Currently, LinkedIn doesn't provide much data to show how this breaks down. On your landing page you can see how many people are in the first three degrees of your network:

---

17. http://tinyurl.com/aydcd
en.wikipedia.org/wiki/Six_Degrees_of_Kevin_Bacon

① Your Connections Your trusted friends and colleagues		1,162
② Two degrees away Friends of friends; each connected to one of your connections		356,400+
③ Three degrees away Reach these users through a friend and one of their friends		9,180,500+
Total users you can contact through an Introduction		9,538,100+

Figure 11: First Three Degrees of Connections

This picture shows my network when I had 243 first degree connections, which means I should know (or have a relationship with) 243 people. I should be able to contact more than 2.4 million people through those 243 contacts. The 243 people are my first degree connections, the 71,900+ are my second degree connections, and the 2.4M people in my third degree connections. My network represented over ¼ of the entire LinkedIn network!

Let's break down what a degree of separation is. Everyone who is in your immediate network is a first degree connection. Everyone who is a first degree connection to one of your first degree contacts is your second degree contact. And their first degree connections are your third degree contacts. You have certain privileges with your first degree contacts that you don't have with contacts beyond the first degree. If you want similar privileges for contacts beyond the first degree you'll need to upgrade your account (or invite them to connect with you and become a first degree). For example, I can see a third degree contact's Profile but I cannot see their email address. I have to use LinkedIn tools to actually contact this person. Let's say I want to contact John Smith, who happens to be a third degree contact.

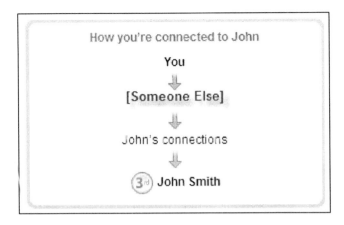

Figure 12: Third-Degree Contact

You can see I'm connected to "John Smith" through someone else (I took the name out for privacy). Instead of showing me John Smith's contact information, it shows me who I know who knows him. I would contact the person I'm connected with through LinkedIn with a note that explains why I want to contact John, and an introduction note for John. My contact could then pass this on to his contact, and eventually to John.

If each person in this chain is comfortable with our relationship, they will likely pass the requests on. It should carry some weight since it is coming through a trusted contact. I think this is a great idea but it has two issues:

First, there is no guarantee I have strong relationships with my connections. I personally haven't met many of my first degree contacts.

Second, the request travels electronically and someone in the chain might not receive it in a timely manner. If it takes two days for each person to get their email and forward it on, it might be six days before an introduction request is even received by the end recipient! If you are in a hurry, it might be best to just pick up the phone.

There is nothing wrong with looking at your first degree contacts' connections to see if there are people you want to create a relationship with, and then invite them to become a first degree connection to you (unfortunately, the ability to change someone from a second or third degree connection to a first degree connection makes it impossible to track the history of the relationship). Make sure that you are actually developing relationships, otherwise this can be seen as spam and get your account suspended. Definitely use custom invitations, not the canned invitation, if you approach your second and third degree contacts to connect with you.

The degrees of separation measurement is helpful but it's just one metric. Don't confuse the size, width or depth of your network with the strength of your network. Amongst the factors to think about, perhaps the most notable is the strength of the relationship you have with each person (something that is not trackable or measured in LinkedIn).

Chapter Summary

- The degrees of separation concept gives you the ability to see how big your first, second and third degree networks are.

- When searching for new contacts, you can easily see how you can get to know them through your connections, and how close they are to you.

8 Recommendations

LinkedIn Recommendations are professional, third-party endorsements for people. Getting a Recommendation on LinkedIn is interesting because your contact enters the Recommendation and you can choose to show or not show the Recommendation—but you can't change it! There is a certain level of credibility to the Recommendation because you can't add or edit Recommendations on your own Profile.

Here's how Recommendations work (I suggest you actually recommend someone in your network). I find a contact I want to recommend and go to their Profile page. I click on the link that says, "Recommend this person." I'm then prompted to say whether I am a colleague, a service provider or a business partner (which means "neither of the other two"). I usually choose business partner since this is the closest description of the relationships with most of my contacts.

Figure 13: Recommend Contact

The next page asks me to clarify the relationship, where I choose my title and her title when we knew each other (or worked with one another). This is one of the clumsiest parts of the process for me because I've met lots of my contacts through networking events and volunteering to work together, not because of some official capacity. I choose the closest "right answer" so I can get to the actual Recommendation.

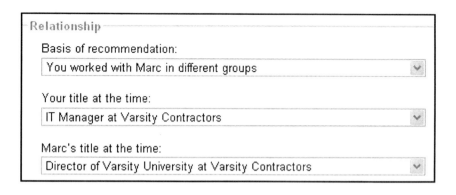

Figure 14: Clarify Relationship

The next box is where you write your Recommendation. I have rarely seen a Recommendation more than one paragraph and think that one paragraph is probably just the right length. If you can imagine finding someone's Profile that is already lengthy, and then finding a lot of wordy Recommendations, you would likely move on to the next one and not even read the entire page! Here's a Recommendation I created for one of my contacts:

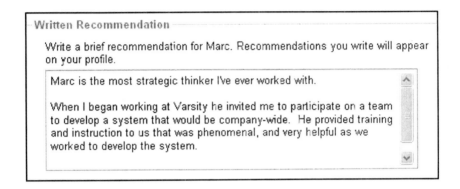

Figure 15: Written Recommendation

After you write the Recommendation and hit "send," your contact will get an email that allows them to show it on their Profile:

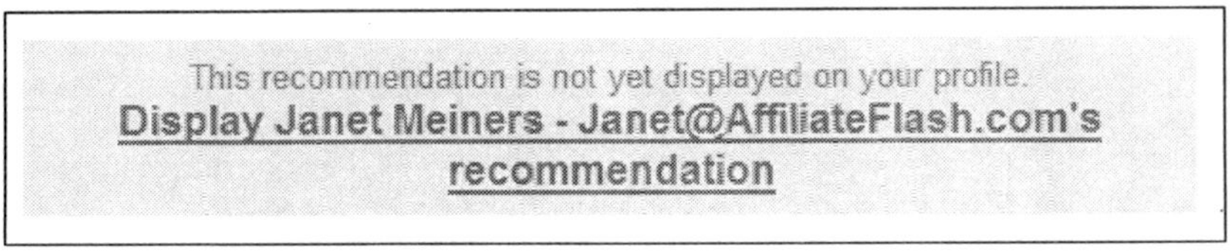

Figure 16: Display Recommendation

When you get an email like this, you click on this link and are taken to a LinkedIn page where you can choose to show or hide the Recommendation. It is not unheard of to ask for a "replacement"...it's like getting a letter of recommendation that isn't quite "right" and asking for the person to redo it (I've done that before).

Figure 17: Show/Hide Recommendation

One of the best ways to get a Recommendation is to recommend someone. Don't give Recommendations that are too general or casual—these are valuable endorsements used for business purposes. If you want specific details in Recommendations you receive, make sure you include specific details in the Recommendations you give. The value of Recommendations diminishes as they are treated as simple, useless comments. This is one reason why you are allowed to hide Recommendations from others.

TIP: If you want a Recommendation, give a Recommendation! You are more likely to get a good Recommendation if you give one first.

Just as you might ask for a letter of recommendation from a prior boss or coworker, I think it is okay to ask for specific wording in a LinkedIn Recommendation. When Janet was preparing my Recommendation she asked me if there was anything specific she should mention. This is an excellent time to communicate your brand to your contact, so make sure you reply with things they could emphasize. This will make your Recommendation more relevant and have the added benefit of conveying your brand to that contact again.

　　　　　　　　　　　　　Chapter 8: Recommendations

If you are working on beefing up the Recommendations on your own Profile there are two things to consider:

First, it is uncommon for someone to have 100% of their contacts give them Recommendations. I have seen discussions where people say others are obviously fishing too much for Recommendations because the percentage of contacts who recommend them is too high. I don't think you should discourage Recommendations, and am not sure how I feel about "too many Recommendations," but I have seen the issue come up.

Second, I have seen a few Profiles of people who are in a job search with a high percentage of Recommendations from coworkers at their last job. I knew there had been recent layoffs and the fact that these people had a dozen or more Recommendations from coworkers (and executives) at one company, and no Recommendations from anyone in their other companies, seemed fake.

Recommendations can be powerful and a great way to reach out to a contact and strengthen your relationship. I don't think you can really do this wrong, as long as you remember this is more of a professional network than a social network. Keeping the tone of Recommendations similar to what you would see in a letter of recommendation ensures your Recommendations are valuable. For an excellent primer on how to write effective Recommendations, visit Naina Redhu's blog post[18]— as a bonus she describes how to write a mediocre and a least effective Recommendation.

Here are my five top recommendations regarding Recommendations:

1. only ask for Recommendations from someone who can give you a real Recommendation
2. only give Recommendations when you have something you can honestly say about the person
3. give Recommendations without demanding a reciprocal Recommendation

---

18. http://tinyurl.com/2rx7uk
aside.in/blog/networking/2006/10/02/linkedin-recommendation-examples/

4. don't feel strong-armed to give a Recommendation

5. give Recommendations that are specific, speaking to professional competencies, skills, attributes, etc.

Chapter Summary

- Getting Recommendations added to your Profile is a great way to substantiate your strengths.

- Giving Recommendations is an excellent way to reach out to your contacts and strengthen the relationships.

- It is okay to ask for Recommendations, just as you might ask for a letter of recommendation from a boss.

- It is okay to ask for revisions in a Recommendation, especially if the Recommendation isn't in line with your branding strategy.

- Write Recommendations that are specific and professionally endorsing, not vague.

- Consider how you grow your own collection of Recommendations, and choose a strategy that works best for you.

"It's what you do and how you leverage your LinkedIn Profile that makes you who you are to your network, and be memorable for time to come."
-- Dan Schawbel, http://www.PersonalBrandingBlog.com

"Meaningful endorsements from people you have worked with in a team or done projects for are the primary validation currency of positive attitude and achievements. It is the most important cutting edge tool for identification of these positive leadership traits. When hiring managers look at resumes, reading LinkedIn endorsements should always be the next tool used to narrow the pile."
-- David Dalka, Senior Marketing and Business Development Professional, http://www.daviddalka.com

---

9 Jobs and Hiring

The Jobs & Hiring section is LinkedIn's job board. A major benefit of Jobs & Hiring is that you can see your relationship with the people who post the jobs—how many degrees away they are from you, how many Recommendations they have, etc. I really like the idea that a person's name is associated with each job posting, which means I can figure out how I might get to know that person better. LinkedIn also shows whether the poster is a hiring manager, recruiter, or HR professional, which is terrific information I rarely see elsewhere!

Last year I did a search for jobs in New York City and saw that there are 415 job postings (across all industries and titles). This year I did a similar search and found 715 jobs in the New York City area. I can see who posted each job and how I'm connected to them (the order I selected was by "Degrees away from you"). We're told to network our way into companies, right? LinkedIn gives us the information we need to do that! Simply search for the name you see next to the job post you like, and you can determine how to network into that person. Alternatively, click on the job title and then you'll see a link to their Profile.

The Jobs page also shows me how many connections I have inside the hiring company. When I click on a job I'm interested in, I see a box that says "Inside connections to the company," which shows me ways I can network into this company.

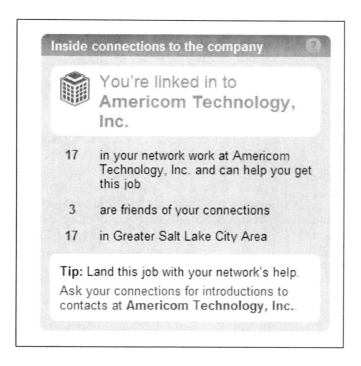

Figure 18: Job Posting Inside Connections

Imagine if every job posting you looked at on Monster told you exactly who you need to talk to and let you know who you might know (or could know, with an Introduction) to network your way closer to that job!

The Jobs section allows you to apply for the job within LinkedIn, with the ability to add a cover letter and upload a resume. When you apply, your *LinkedIn Profile* is sent to the person at that company (recruiter, hiring manager, HR, or whoever put the job posting up). Yet another reason to ensure your Profile is filled in with good details.

I like how simple the interface is and how much information you get on each job. With over 40,000 job boards out there it is confusing to know what tools you should be using. Because the networking information is tied directly into each job search result I would strongly suggest the LinkedIn job section be one of the job boards you check regularly.

There are some improvements that LinkedIn can make to the user experience here:

1. **Include salary as a search criterion** - You can filter the search results based on location, experience level, when the job was posted, title, company, function and industry, but it would be nice to be able to filter the results based on salary range. I should note this feature isn't very common in other search engines, but would really help job seekers know what jobs they should even apply to.

2. **Allow me to save my searches** - Whether there is a "save search" button that saves the criteria within my Profile in LinkedIn, or the option to take an RSS feed (which I can then use in other systems like Google Reader or JibberJobber), the save search function makes it convenient and quick for me to recheck postings I might be interested in.

3. **Send me email alerts of jobs based on my criteria** - Most job boards today allow you to save a job search and have results emailed to you daily or weekly. This is a standard job board feature and would make the user experience much richer.

4. **Get more job postings** - In the Greater Salt Lake area there were only 8 job listings last year (when I searched), compared with 12 this time I searched, and in New York City there were fewer than 500 last year (just over 700 this year). I know there are a lot more jobs out there. If LinkedIn can figure out how to get more postings (and keep the postings real), this would be the first place I would come to look for a job!

Here's a bonus idea for using job boards like this, whether you are looking for a job or not. If you are involved in a business that has competitors, or want to do research on a company's competitors, use job boards to see what activity is happening at the competition!

If you find they are hiring two new key roles in their customer service department you could guess they really are having customer issues. If they are hiring ten new sales executives in New England, you know they are growing in a new area! Job boards may not have the best record for landing a job, but they are rich with competitive intelligence information!

Chapter Summary

- LinkedIn Jobs shows you the people in your network that have some tie to any particular job, which can help you network your way into a company.

- Use LinkedIn Jobs to do competitive intelligence research, whether you are looking for a job, looking for a customer, or just checking out your competition.

10 Companies

When I wrote the first edition of this book, researching companies was limited to whatever you could find when doing a People search. In the last year, LinkedIn has added several enhancements. The addition of Companies, which is one of four menu items at the top, is one of the most powerful features LinkedIn has to offer. Why? Because you can do some significant research on companies, and even network your way into them, within LinkedIn. Let's explore a few ways to get value out of Companies.

When you click on the Companies link at the top menu you are taken to the Companies search page where you can search by industry, country or zip code (postal code), or by company name. You will see a list of "companies in your network," based on the degree of separation of the contact(s) in that company, and be able to browse industries that are in the database.

A current limitation of the search results is that companies in the database are provided by Capital IQ,[19] which means that not all companies are in the system. For now you can't add your own company to the database—it has to come from the Capital IQ database. LinkedIn says they have plans in the future to allow you to add companies to the system.

Another way to find company information is to check Profiles for a hyperlinked company name. An easy example is IBM; if you do a search for someone who lists IBM as a company they used to work at, IBM should be hyperlinked (again, depending on whether Capital IQ sent that data to LinkedIn). If you aren't sure what company you want to look at, or network into, think about the type of person (titles, roles, where they are located, etc.) and you might find some companies that would be great target companies.

Click on a company you want information on. You'll see a summary, provided by Capital IQ. The summary states whether that company has a parent company, where company employees worked before they joined that company ("career path for [company name] employees before"), who is in your network that is tied to the company (shows you contacts in your first three degrees), new hires, promotions or job changes, key statistics, and more. Not only are you getting a rich summary of company information for your target company, you also learn who you are already connected with that might help you get into a key contact at that company! This is a powerful benefit of using LinkedIn, and—if you are in sales, looking for partners, a job seeker or whatever—a compelling reason to increase your network strategically.

Creating a successful companies strategy on LinkedIn will depend on knowing what you are looking for. You don't have to know the company names, although if you do it's easy to do research on that company and to network your way in (unless, of course, the company is not in the database yet).

---

19. http://tinyurl.com/linkedin-data
linkedin.custhelp.com/cgi-bin/linkedin.cfg/php/enduser/popup_adp.php?p
_sid=U3g22-hj&p_lva=&p_li=&p_faqid=358&p_created=1206040676&p_
sp=cF9zcmNoPTEmcF9zb3J0X2J5PWRmbHQ6MSZwX2dyaWRzb3J0P
SZwX3Jvd19jbnQ9MTYsMTYmcF9wcm9kcz0wJnBfY2F0cz0mcF9wdj0
mcF9jdj0mcF9zZWFyY2hfdHlwZT1hbnN3ZXJzLnNlYXJjaaF9ubCZwX3Bh
Z2U9MSZwX3NlYXJjaaF90ZXh0PWFkZCZwBteSBjb21wYW55

If you have an email address provided by a company with a presence on LinkedIn, you can access the "Company Group." Once you leave a company and update your profile you are automatically removed from the Group. Company Groups allow you to do four things:

1. Search and view other members in the Company network
2. Provide a status for coworkers (members in the Company network)
3. Get news relevant to your company
4. Ask questions in the Q&A to members in the Company network

It's like a social environment, provided by LinkedIn, for current company employees. I don't know how valuable this is for members of Company Groups, but if your company has a Group you might consider checking it out.

Aside from the "Companies" section of LinkedIn, where the data comes from Capital IQ, you do have the ability to get your company listed in the Services Providers directory. Simply ask a contact to give you a recommendation and choose "Service Provider" as the type of relationship, and you'll show up as a Service Provider.

The idea behind LinkedIn Services is that you can find service providers who come recommended by other LinkedIn users. You can view service providers by categories (graphic/web designer, attorney or handyman) and sort the results by who recommends them (connections that are your first degree, second degree or recommended by anyone in LinkedIn).

There are a lot of places on the Internet to look for service providers (search for "find service provider" and you'll get a ton of hits); the common search engine would be the most popular. However, I think finding a good service provider online is far from perfect. Many of the trusted service providers I use don't even have a web presence.

LinkedIn allows me to see how I am connected to the service provider and see what others have to say about their company (in the Recommendations on that individual). When I search for a house cleaner it shows me house cleaners who have been recommended by anyone in LinkedIn. I can choose to see house cleaners recommended by my first degree contacts (there aren't any house cleaners that my first degree contacts recommend), and then second degree contacts. There are four house cleaners that my second degree contacts recommend and I can see who they are and what my contacts, and others, say about them.

Assuming all of my connections are based on trust (or I have some kind of relationship with each connection), recommendations to service providers should carry some weight. When I first learned about this I thought, "Whom do I know that I could recommend?" My principal business is the JibberJobber website, and I don't think a website is a good candidate for a service provider. But I am also a speaker and speakers could greatly benefit from having Recommendations which put them in the Service Provider section of LinkedIn. Also, I have associates who would benefit from an honest Recommendation. It is a courteous and helpful gesture to give a Recommendation whenever possible, as that might help their business grow. It is also an excellent way to make you more memorable to your service provider contacts, who are more likely to remember you, consider the Recommendation a favor, and be willing to take action on your behalf in the future.

As you connect with lawyers, accountants, mechanics, consultants and other service providers, think about how you could recommend or endorse them. If you provide services, or if it makes sense for you to show up in the Service Provider directory, ask your contacts to choose "service provider" when they give you a Recommendation.

There's a significant difference between what you see in the Companies search results and what you see in the Service Providers directory.

Chapter Summary

- Companies have data that comes from Capital IQ and is merged with information from your network, providing you a rich tool for research.

- Find companies of interest using the Company search page or by finding companies whose names are hyperlinked from Profiles.

- Learn about your target company and determine how you could network your way into the company, or strengthen your contacts in that company, based on who is already in your network.

- If you work at a company that is in the Companies database, consider joining its Company Group for collaboration and communication with other LinkedIn users who are at the same company.

- Periodically check the services section to see if there are service-providers that you can use (or see if your competition is listed).

- If your service provider is on LinkedIn, endorse their services, which can help them in their marketing strategy.

- Coach your contacts, as they give you a Recommendation, so that you can show up in the Service Provider directory.

"The Company Profile pages on LinkedIn are GOLD for anyone using LinkedIn to research companies, individuals or positions within a company—and for Recruiters searching for candidates! The Company Profile page contains a wealth of information on the company via Business Week and employment data compiled from the information current and former employee have entered in LinkedIn. This market intelligence is fantastic, allowing you to see hiring and promotional activity within the company, as well as quick links to additional information to research competitors, similar companies, etc. As a Recruiter and avid networker, this is one of my favorite features within LinkedIn, and it can be used for business development and job search purposes in the same way."
-- Jennifer McClure, Executive Recruiter/Executive Coach,
http://www.cincyrecruiter.com

LinkedIn Groups

When I first wrote this book, I wasn't too keen on Groups. Groups didn't have a search feature and there was no way for Group members to communicate with other Group members (except one-by-one).

In 2008 a number of new features were introduced[20] that really make Groups a must-see feature. I've heard people talk about some of the features with so much excitement they've shadowed the power of Answers, which is significant!

Let's talk about what Groups is. There are over 90,000 Groups in LinkedIn. There are Groups for alumni associations, special interests, companies, industries, types of people, etc. When I find a Group I want to join I simply click the "Join this group" link. The Group manager decides, from the Group admin page, who to let into the Group, but you won't get a notification unless you email them asking to join the Group. I get this type of "please let me join your Group email" regularly with my JibberJobber Career Management Group.[21]

---

20. http://blog.linkedin.com/2008/08/28/post-3-2
21. http://www.linkedin.com/e/gis/5908

Once you join the Group, you have access to browse through and search the members. You can message members directly, and view their Profiles. In the Advanced People Search you have the option to include members of your Groups in the search results (whether they are connected to you or not). Since you can include Group members in search results, even if they are not in your network, you increase your chances of being found by people outside of your network, based on the Groups you belong to.

A powerful new feature in Groups includes the ability to start or participate in Discussions with other Group members. Go to the Group page and click on the Discussions tab, where you can post any topic you want. Be careful to keep it on-message, and on-brand for who you are! The ability to create Discussions is almost like having a mini-blog, or asking a question in Answers, but it's limited to Group members. This is a terrific addition to Groups, and allows you to find more experts, and develop your own brand, amongst a specific subset of LinkedIn users—members of the Group who should have similar professional interests or something else in common.

Another new feature in Groups is the ability to share News items. You simply click on the News tab, and enter a URL to share with others. If you have a blog post or press release you want to share, you can do it from here. I would caution you to not submit every blog post you write, or your News submissions will likely start to look like spam and be disregarded. News items can also have comments, which makes it similar to the Discussion functionality.

As a Group member I can choose to show the Group logo on my LinkedIn Profile, as well as in the search results when my Profile shows up. I can show my support, or affinity, for certain causes, associations, groups, clubs, companies, etc. caution you to not show too many, as it can just add noise to your Profile, and make people wonder about your overall strategy ("How can he possibly belong to 50 Groups? And why is he in a women's Group?").

To optimize your strategy on LinkedIn, I recommend you look for all relevant Groups you can join. I don't recommend adding them all to your Profile page, as that would only clutter your Profile. Joining relevant Groups will help you increase your search and searchability (ability to "find and be found") with those Group members, and enable you to be involved in relevant discussions.

Starting your own Group is really easy. Simply go to the Groups page and click on the "Create a Group" tab. Before you create a Group you'll want to have a name and description for it, as well as a logo. Then, the key is to let people know about the Group. You can let all of your network contacts, clients, and prospects know about the Group through your email signature, on your website or blog, in newsletters, in comments you leave on other blogs, in Group discussions etc. Be careful to not come across as a self-promotional spammer, as no one wants to read spam messages, and anybody perceived as a spammer is quickly ignored.

If you describe your Group well when you set it up you'll have people find it as they search for Groups. For example, I did not describe my Group well enough, so if you search for "job search" you won't see my Group. Make sure your description includes words that people might search for as they look for your Group. When LinkedIn announced they were going to introduce the Group search function, they announced they had over 90,000 Groups, and I saw an increase in the number of members requesting to join my Group. I rarely advertise it anywhere, so I know most people are coming to my Group either through the search results or because they see the logo on other Profiles.

One of the benefits of owning a Group is the ability to spread your Group virally. First, as I mentioned, people can come across your Group if Group members opt to put your logo on their Profile. Many of my JibberJobber Career Management members have the JibberJobber logo on their Profile. Aside from advertising the Group to anyone who views their Profile, they are also advertising my company (the JibberJobber logo is spelled out in the logo). I created the Group with the hope that I'd essentially get my logo plastered on a Profile, kind of like a bumper sticker. Another way your Group spreads virally is when someone joins the Group. When their connections log in to LinkedIn, on the home page, they see what's new in their network, including any Groups that their contacts join. Each time someone joins your Group there's a chance some of their contacts will learn about your Group, and will see a hyperlink they can click on to join.

In the first edition of this book, I highlighted significant differences between Yahoo! Groups and LinkedIn Groups. Yahoo! Groups are well known as email forums, also referred to as listservs, and have been around for a long time. Over the years I've been on a number of Yahoo! Groups, and currently belong to about 30. For me, the most valuable aspect of a Yahoo! Group is that I get communication from Group members right in my inbox, and I don't have to log in to the site to have a conversation. They provide other features, but I'm guessing the email functionality is the most useful function they offer.

LinkedIn Groups, at the time I first wrote this book, had no collaboration or communication that was group-wide. If I wanted to communicate with Group members as a group, whether I was a member or the owner, it was impossible. It was a considerable weakness in using LinkedIn Groups and I commented that having a LinkedIn Group complementing a Yahoo! Group would be a comprehensive solution.

That has changed. Today, I still favor the ease-of-use and convenience factors I have with Yahoo! Groups, and will not be leaving my Yahoo! Groups anytime soon, but with the recent introduction of LinkedIn Group discussions, and sharing news events, I think you can get away with creating a Group on LinkedIn without needing a complementary Yahoo! Group. As a member who has something to say (a brand, expertise or opinion to share), it's a great opportunity to communicate your message to a targeted audience. In fact, it may be more effective to join the right Groups and participate in Group discussions than to have an Answers strategy, because your questions on Answers go out to your network, whereas your questions or messages on Discussions go out to those who join the Group where the discussion is. In other words, people who have an interest in the Group topic would have an in interest in your message, as long as it was aligned with the purpose of the Group. I'm not advocating an either/or strategy with Answers and Discussions, as I would encourage you to use both tools, but you can see that each has it's advantages.

Also, I'm not saying Yahoo! Groups are now defunct or useless, but they are not as necessary as you create your Group strategy. Yahoo! Groups are still useful, and have their pros and cons when compared with LinkedIn Groups. And, in an interesting turn-of-events, I recently learned that Yahoo! Groups is putting some features in place to add more social functionality, which might change it's perceived value as only an email listserv.

Let's wrap this up. As a user of LinkedIn, I encourage you to:

- Seek out and join Groups where your peers and target audience are. You can join up to 50 Groups, but don't show all 50 Group logos on your Profile, as it will just clutter your Profile.

- As you need to grow your network and meet new people, go into your Groups, browse the members, or do searches from Advanced People Search (include the Groups) or from the Group itself.

- Reach out to Group members by sending them individual messages, ensuring you have a purpose and reason to reach out to them.

- Find Discussions you can join, or start Discussions and share news items with the entire Group. Pay attention to what you say, and how you say it, and avoid any netiquette missteps.

If you are interested in owning a Group, I encourage you to:

- If you haven't yet, go to Groups and click on the Create a Group tab and get started on your own Group.

- Market your Group, if appropriate, in as many places as you can. This includes your email signature, on blogs and websites, in comments you leave on other blogs, in newsletters, etc.

- Figure out how open your Group is. If it's an alumni Group, you'll likely want to limit access to alumni of the school or company. If it's a special interest Group you may be more open. Determine how open you'll be based on how much administration you want to do (do you want to have to check out each applicant to join the Group before you approve them?).

- Regularly spend time managing the Discussions and News items submitted to keep out spam and weird messaging while encouraging conversations on other, more appropriate messages.

- Communicate to Group members by initiating Discussions or news items OR exporting the Group list and sending an email to the Group outside of LinkedIn.

I'm very impressed with the changes in Groups this last year, as it really adds value to my LinkedIn experience, and allows me to enhance my LinkedIn strategy. My Group has around 1,000 members, while other Groups, like Execunet's Group,[22] has over 90,000 members. It's interesting to see the quantity and quality of messages coming through each Group, and I would encourage you to not discount joining smaller Groups as your voice might not get lost in the noise of a larger Group. Can you see how Groups could be an essential part of your LinkedIn strategy?

Chapter Summary

- Join Groups where your peers or target audience are. Consider adding certain, perhaps not all, Group logos to your Profile.

- Communicate with other Group members using the Discussion and news sharing tools.

- Browse and search through Group members to see if there are contacts who should be in your network, or contacts you should initiate a discussion with.

- Consider starting your own Group for your company, profession, industry, passion, local geographic area, etc. As Group owner, understand the obligations and issues you will deal with.

- Consider the value a complementary Yahoo! Group could offer you.

---

22. http://www.linkedin.com/static?key=execunet_landing_5

"Administering a LinkedIn Group is a terrific way to subtly raise awareness of yourself. It's a fairly simple process to start a Group. Perhaps the most difficult part is designing your Group's logo. I started and manage three Groups, one for my high school and two for my geographic area, and I can see that most people who join them review my LinkedIn Profile. That puts me in front of many people who may never have been aware of me otherwise. It also gives me the opportunity to welcome them and reach out to them as potential connections. It can work for you too, so consider what need is unfulfilled and start your own LinkedIn Group."
-- **Christine Pilch, Co-owner of Grow My Company and co-author of "Understanding Brand Strategies: The Professional Service Firm's Guide to Growth."**
http://www.GrowMyCo.com

"Everyone knows that it's a good thing to network but most people don't do it unless they need something. Building a LinkedIn network is a little like that. You really won't appreciate just how valuable your network has become until you need it. My advice is to start now! Take Jason's recommendations to heart and get going. When the time comes you will be glad that you did."
-- **Simon Meth,** http://www.martinandsimon.com **and**
http://www.ere.net/blogs/sittingxlegged

12 LinkedIn Answers

LinkedIn Answers may be one of the most intriguing features that LinkedIn has to offer. With LinkedIn Answers, you post a question and invite your network to respond. Questions can be seen by second and third degree connections. Questions posted are extremely diverse, ranging from knowledge-based issues to help in finding a job or resources. Questions are usually appropriate for the type of people you find on LinkedIn.

When LinkedIn first launched Answers there was a lot of concern about users spamming their networks with sales, MLM, job postings, and more. LinkedIn did a decent job of putting in various controls to reduce the spam potential. It's in their best interest to make Answers as valuable and effective as possible.

One of the controls to keep the spammers out is the limit to how many questions you can ask each month. Currently the limit is 10 questions per calendar month (if you upgrade you can ask 25 questions each month), which should encourage you to think about the questions you have and ask only the best, or most important. Of course, you can answer as many questions as you want.

There are a handful of LinkedIn users who regularly answer over 150 questions each month. You can see these people, in the This Week's Top Experts section, on the front page of Answers, below the five questions shown. In order to get listed here you have to receive the "best answer" designation on questions you answer.

TIP: Try to ask a question at least once a month. This will give you the opportunity to intelligently probe your contacts in a creative way.

When you submit a question you can choose up to 200 people from your first degree network to email. I recommend using this email notifier to invite your contacts to answer the question. It's more likely that your network finds out about the question via email than by seeing it on their LinkedIn home page. In my experience I'll get more responses if I choose 200 contacts than if I don't have the system email them. If I don't have the system email them I still get a pretty good response from people whom I don't really know, but that's probably because of the size of my network.

Each question is open for a certain period of time, currently seven days. During the seven days anyone logged into LinkedIn can answer the question. At the end of the seventh day it closes and no one can answer it. The question and answers remain available as archived records. If you have a good question that received good answers, you might consider opening it again (after it closes). For example, I asked a question, got great answers, and then reopened it for another period. I was able to choose up to 100 first degree contacts to get the question emailed to them. This is effective as my network is larger than 200, and not all of my contacts got the question emailed to them the first time.

During the seven days that your question is open you can do things such as clarify your question, close it, choose a best answer, etc. If you need to clarify the question I recommend just appending text at the end instead of changing the entire question—that way if someone has answered the original question their answer will still make sense.

What a terrific source of knowledge! Answers has the added benefit of allowing you to learn about each participant and determine how qualified they are to answer your question. With one click you are led to their Profile.

Once the question is closed you should choose the "good" and "best" answers. As you do this you are reaching out to your contacts, endorsing what they say, thanking them for contributing, and putting your brand in front of them again. You are also building the credibility of the person who answered, as their Profile will display how many "best answers" they have contributed. LinkedIn gives people "expert" status as they get more and more "best answer" votes. This system is similar to eBay's system which allows users to build credibility for one another as they rank them, and it's a way to develop your brand through LinkedIn.

If you ask a question that others consider inappropriate (like asking a question that is a job posting, and not saying that it's a job posting) then they may flag it. This peer monitoring is another control that LinkedIn introduced to help eliminate spam. It seems that your question will remain up unless it is flagged too many times, or if the LinkedIn staff reviews it and determines that it should be taken down. Be careful how you word questions (and your answers to other people's questions)! The LinkedIn policy can change quickly, but no matter what, you don't want to brand yourself as a spammer with your network contacts.

If you are using LinkedIn to develop your personal brand, or a company brand, I encourage you to have an Answers strategy. At a minimum, you should be asking questions once a month. While you can ask more than once a week, I don't recommend it (unless you email different groups each time). If you really want to get your brand out there, look for questions you can respond to on a daily basis. LinkedIn Answers makes this easy if you use an RSS reader, as you can subscribe to an RSS feed by category. Instead of logging in to LinkedIn on a regular basis to see what new questions are there, simply follow the feed and they will be sent to your RSS reader.

The key to an effective, aggressive Answers strategy is to not pitch your offerings, or come across as too self-promotional. Every question you ask, and answer you give, should help develop you as a subject matter expert, or as a thought leader, or else you will lose credibility and start to look like a spammer. I think it's appropriate to leave links in your questions or answers, even to the point where you could create a blog post just so you can link back to it, but it all has to add value to the discussion. Sharing knowledge is what we're after, and as you share more pertinent knowledge you can be seen as the subject matter expert that you are.

TIP: Try to answer a question at least once a month, which will give you visibility to the LinkedIn community.

Chapter Summary

- Participating in Answers is an excellent way to make new contacts as well as quantify your personal brand.

- Make sure you participate intelligently and really add value to the questions and answers.

- Your Answers strategy can include just asking questions, just answering questions, or a combination.

"When you ask a question on the 'Answers' forum take the time to thank each person who tried to help. Then remember to close and rate the question. People have taken the time to help you; it is simple common courtesy to thank them."
-- Sheilah Etheridge, owner of SME Management

"Use the questions and answers feature to start conversations, create community, and position yourself as a subject matter expert. By answering questions, you are simultaneously endorsing your candidacy and expertise."
-- Barbara Safani, http://www.CareerSolvers.com

Part III
Wrapping it Up

There's more to a rich LinkedIn experience than what you can find on their website. Part 3 introduces you to using LinkedIn for your personal branding strategy, warns you about shady practices that you might encounter, shares some thoughts on netiquette, talks about resources complementary to LinkedIn and this book, and leaves you with some final thoughts.

13 LinkedIn for Personal Branding

LinkedIn is a personal tool—your account is yours and yours alone (well, unless you sign up with a company email!). It is not a bulletin board for a company, although you can put language on your Profile that explains what your company does. People use LinkedIn to help their current situation (for example, asking a question in Answers that addresses a particular job-related need). Did you know it's also a great tool to quantify and build your personal professional brand?

Developing and sharing a strong personal brand is not as easy as throwing a Profile up. You should think about what your personal brand currently is (everyone has a brand, whether they like it or not), what it should be, and how you can strengthen it, online and offline.

This book is not a personal branding book, so I won't cover the topics of who you are, who you should be and all the ways to quantify your brand online. I will share some ideas on personal branding specific to LinkedIn. If you are interested in personal branding I highly suggest Career Distinction, which has been called the bible of personal branding. You can learn more at:

http://www.CareerDistinction.com. Other excellent personal branding resources include http://www.PersonalBrandingBlog.com and http://www.PersonalBrandingSummit.com.

Here are steps I recommend you take, as you work on your personal brand using LinkedIn:

First, make sure you are showing the right information on your Private Profile and your Public Profile. LinkedIn allows you to view your Profile as others would see it, and you can always log out to see what your Profile looks like to those that are not logged in. Are the Profiles showing enough information? Are they showing too much information? My experience with Public Profiles is that too many only show a name and title (or something similar—too little information). I rarely take the time to login to view your full Profile. If you want to advertise who you are and why you are valuable, make it easy for people to learn about you without logging in!

Second, change your Public Profile URL from the default assigned value (which looks like gibberish) to something more descriptive of who you are. For example, you can see that my Public Profile ends in "jas-onalba" instead of something like "/1/234/698"—so when people see a link to my Profile they know exactly where they are going:

Figure 19: Edit Profile

This image is from the Profile edit screen, where they show you your Public Profile URL—to change it all you need to do is click on the Edit link. Please don't put something regretful, like "hairylegs." If you want to do that, go get an account on MySpace where that's accept-able—doing that on LinkedIn will not be considered cute—and I'm pretty sure you'll regret it later.

Third, share your LinkedIn Profile. The easiest, most effective and most viral way of sharing your personal brand via your LinkedIn Profile is to put the URL in your email signature. Every time someone reads your email signature they'll know they can learn more about where you've been and what you've done (if your Public Profile is done right). Each time your emails get forwarded more people will see your Profile. Another way to share your Profile is to put the "View My LinkedIn Profile" image on your personal website or blog.

I should note that I do not have my LinkedIn URL in my email signatures. I have a few websites and blogs I want people to go to, and feel it is better to put those URLs in my signature, than to have one more link. If you have a website, or blog, or any other web property that you'd rather send people to, you obviously don't have to put your LinkedIn URL in the signature. My decision was based on keeping my signature as clean as possible and pointing people to where I want them to end up. You have to make your own decision, which will be easy if you don't have a website!

I attended a presentation for job seekers about "regaining your identity" where the speaker talked about using resumes in networking events. He said employed professionals don't pass out resumes, they hand out business cards. If you get a resume from someone, you have a preconceived idea about what they want (a job, right? Isn't that what a resume says?). However, if you get a business card from someone you have a different idea of what they want, or can offer.

This concept transfers quite nicely to the LinkedIn Profile. If you send your resume out with every single email you send you will probably get into trouble with your employer. Sending a resume says "I'm looking, if you can help then let me know." However, sending a link to your LinkedIn Profile says "Here's my professional profile, check it out." Your LinkedIn Profile can be identical to your resume, with the same quantifying statements and other information commonly found in a resume. But the fact that you are just pointing someone to your online Profile sends a different message.

Finally, if you leave a comment on a blog, online newspaper, forum or some other website, you have two opportunities to leave your LinkedIn Profile URL. This is especially applicable if you don't have your own website or blog (in which case you might prefer to leave your website or blog URL). The first place to put your LinkedIn Profile URL is in the "website" box, if there is one. Usually, when you leave a comment they ask for your name, email address and website.

Chapter Summary

- There are various things you can do within LinkedIn to strengthen your personal brand, and take advantage of LinkedIn's search engine optimization.

- Your LinkedIn Profile is kind of like a resume, without any of the negative connotations that a resume might have.

- Use your Public Profile URL as your "website" address when you comment on blogs.

14 | Shady Practices

With over twenty-eight million users in LinkedIn, you are almost guaranteed to run into people who don't abide by common netiquette or even the LinkedIn User Agreement. There is a link at the bottom of each page to the User Agreement that I'm sure many people have not read. Even if they have read it, they may take liberties in how they interpret the policies.

Here are some actual practices I consider to be "shady" that have negatively affected people's experience while on LinkedIn:

Email in name field: This is a very simple, almost non-offensive deed but I wanted to bring it out for one reason. It is against the terms set forth in the User Conduct section of the User Agreement:[23] "You understand and agree not to use LinkedIn to:...Post content in fields that aren't intended for that content. Example: Putting an address in a name or title field." This may be the most common offense, to the point where it

---

23. http://tinyurl.com/zl5tl
linkedin.com/static?key=user_agreement&trk=
ftr_useragre

looks like "everyone is doing it," but just realize it is against the rules and may subject your account to be suspended.

Tollboothing: This is when people charge you to have access to their LinkedIn connections. Of course you can still do a search on their network, but if you want an introduction or some other kind of endorsed communication to one of their contacts, they would charge you. The logic behind this is "I put a lot of time and effort into building my network, and this is my livelihood, so you should expect to have to pay me for my services." I don't agree with this behavior. While there are people who agree with it, they are in a small minority. If you are really interested in developing relationships this might be something that will greatly hinder your networking and LinkedIn strategy.

Lying: One of the best ways to be found by companies that hire Yale graduates is to graduate from Yale, right? What if you could just put Yale as one of your schools that you went to? Well, you can. You can lie about places that you worked and where you went to school. You can actually lie about anything on your Profile. This is one reason why the Recommendations carries so much weight, because you can't edit what someone else writes about you. People have been known to put false information on their LinkedIn Profile to increase their chances of being found by recruiters or hiring managers.

Vincent Wright, founder of the MyVirtualPowerForum Yahoo! Group found a Profile where the person had worked for 15 years in 100 different companies. Vincent called him the 1,500 year old man (100 companies x 15 years at each one = 1,500 years of work experience!). It's important to note that Vincent is a professional recruiter—and professional recruiters can smell this type of deception from a mile away. Make sure your Profile is clean and verifiable—just as your resume should be.

What should you do if someone contacts you because of the school or company listed on your account? In an email to MyVirtualPowerForum Scott Allen recommended the following:

"If someone does send you an invitation saying that they're a former colleague or classmate, at a minimum, at least take a look at the dates and other entries on their Profile and make sure they jibe. And if they don't have a full position and description listed, that's a yellow flag too."

It's really up to you to make sure the person you connect with, or respond to, is who he says he is. LinkedIn isn't in the business of providing verified information, so there has to be a certain amount of trust involved. Remember, this is an online environment and there is a lot more to a person and their history than what you'll see on their LinkedIn Profile.

Using LinkedIn Answers to cloak inappropriate questions. The LinkedIn community has been very clear they don't want Answers to turn into a spam-laden area, generating useless requests for information and sending out numerous emails that become a burden to manage. This is not as big an issue as it was when they originally launched because of mechanisms introduced to prevent spam, but there are still people who use it for "thinly veiled advertising, job postings, job search help and the latest trend, people looking for investors." Answers has a purpose. Abusing it not only clutters and diminishes the value of the system, it shows you don't respect others.

Fishing for fake Recommendations. Since you can't make up Recommendations for yourself, and most people won't create fake LinkedIn Profiles and then endorse their main Profile, you might have people ask you for Recommendations. This really isn't a big deal, and is common practice with reference letters. I have asked past coworkers and bosses for letters of recommendation *and even coached them on specifics that I wanted them to bring out.* But there's one big difference—the shady part is when someone you don't really know asks for a Recommendation. It usually comes in the form of "If you recommend me I'll recommend you." My typical response to this type of request is "I don't really feel like I know you well enough to give you a Recommendation—sorry. I'd like to get to know you better before I do that." When I respond like that I never receive a reply!

Light-linking. This refers to linking with anyone who asks for a connection. Many people take a casual position on this (like, open networkers) but it does cut into LinkedIn's value proposition. In other words, the idea of LinkedIn providing me a view of strong networks, based on knowing each contact and having some kind of relationship, is diminished when connections are made with people you don't know well-enough to endorse, recommend, or pass along to another network contact. Of course, you can argue that light-linking is okay as it:

a. expands your network and reach, and

b. increases the chances that you'll be found because your network gets bigger and more diverse.

Fishing for email addresses. Because so many people violate the rule about putting email addresses in the name field, it's quite easy to find email addresses to put into a list. I'm not suggesting that *you* do anything shady, but here's how easy it is. Just search on ".com" in the search box and you'll find as many email addresses as you could ever want. It's that easy to find email addresses to spam!

These are not all of the shady practices—the key is to be cautious.

Chapter Summary

- People will do things wrong, sometimes unknowingly. Beware of who you interact with, and how you interact with them.

- If you violate LinkedIn policy you risk having your account suspended, or being seen as someone that does not respect "the rules."

15 On Netiquette

Even though LinkedIn doesn't have a lot of social interaction with other members built into its user experience, there are plenty of opportunities to practice social guffaws with contacts you develop in LinkedIn. You will be invited to connect with someone else. Some of your connections will ask for (and maybe even merit) a Recommendation. Perhaps you'll be on an email forum where LinkedIn is discussed and you somehow come across as an expert!

It's important to know some basic rules of Internet etiquette. Aside from having an online presence, and developing your personal brand, you should continually portray yourself within the boundaries of your brand. This isn't to say that you should get walked all over, but it's good to understand the basics. Here are some basics to consider:

1. **Be nice and concise.** Always. I think we are in the habit of *skimming* more than reading, mostly because of the massive amount of information we can read. Having a concise message with a nice tone will do wonders for your online brand.

2. **Avoid sarcasm when writing.** Since people are likely to skim your messages and probably not catch every meaning that you intend, think twice about funny jokes and sarcasm you want to slip into your messages. I frequently hit the backspace button when writing many of my emails. While I hate watering down my messages I realize that the jokes or sarcasm would just be a distraction from my real message and could be misinterpreted.

3. **Assume the best when you are reading someone else's communication.** Scott Allen advises people to "presume good intent" when reading an email that might come across as negative, harsh or inappropriate. Scott is right—while you know to be careful when sending messages perhaps your contact didn't get the memo on netiquette. Give them the benefit of the doubt!

4. **Don't chastise or preach.** I've seen too many discussion threads (a string of emails around the same subject) that go from bad to worse. What starts off as a general admonition or knowledge-sharing email easily turns into personal jabs and accusations. You can pursue this path if you want but I've found it's much more effective to just bow out of the discussion and move on to something else. Everyone involved will appreciate the thread dying down and you'll look more mature, wiser, or just smarter for not pursuing an online fist-fight.

5. **Consider cultural differences when reading or writing anything.** Every list I'm on has a good representation of people from all walks of life even from different countries. There are people whose first language is not the same as most others on the list. There are people who are right out of school (or still students) and others are at the end of their career. There are entrepreneurs, executives, artists, rich and poor. All of these things affect the messages and the culture of the list—and will likely lead to misunderstandings. Now you know!

6. **Know when to take it off-list.** Lots of topics are of interest, interesting, and appropriate. However, there are times when it makes sense to take a topic (or thread) offline. If the discussion starts off slightly off-topic and it gets deeper and more technical, take it off-list. If the discussion is between you and one other person, take it off-list. If the discussion is completely off-topic, or personal, take it off-list.

There are always exceptions to the rules, and you'll notice lots of people don't seem to know them! But remember this: everything you write, whether it's a comment, an email, an instant message or anything, may come back to haunt you. In fact, you should write everything with the idea that it will be on the front page of a major newspaper, with full credit back to you!

Liz Ryan's book Happy About Online Networking is a great resource for more information on netiquette. Liz writes about a whole myriad of online environments to network in and how to get the best out of them. Throughout the entire book there are pearls of wisdom on what to do and what not to do, which comes down to "netiquette."

Chapter Summary

- Learning the rules of netiquette will help you maintain the proper relationships as you communicate with people online.

- Understand netiquette mistakes may help you be more understanding or patient with people that don't understand them.

16 Complementary Tools and Resources

As someone who loves and appreciates net-working I must recommend that LinkedIn is only one networking tool you should use. It might be your main online networking tool, but it shouldn't be your only online networking tool. Saying that LinkedIn is the only online network site you should use is like saying you should only attend one face-to-face network event, or join only one club or association. There is immense value in attending different networking events, in different circles, and getting a cross-section or cross-pol-lination in your own network. In that spirit, here are some tools I recommend as complements to LinkedIn.

Many people use LinkedIn to develop an online personal presence as part of their personal branding strategy. This means they develop their Profile much like they would develop a resume, putting their best foot forward and optimizing it so people will

a. find it when searching for keywords (such as "project manager"), and/or

b. be compelled to have interest in working with, hiring or finding out more about the person.

If you are interested in developing an online presence there are other ways to do it. A Public Profile on LinkedIn should be one part of a multifaceted strategy, not your entire strategy. Here's a quick list of excellent (and free) ways to claim your Profile on the Internet, and perhaps even get your name on the front page of search engine results instead of that famous person, author, or blogger whom you share a name with:

- Find other sites to develop profiles, including Jobster.com, Emurse.com, ZoomInfo.com, etc.

- Set up a free blog where you can continually brand yourself and quantify your breadth and depth in regular, valuable blog posts.

- Comment on other blogs to establish a presence and footprint, pointing back to a central place (either your blog or one of your online profiles (like your LinkedIn Public Profile).

- Develop a Squidoo lens where you can list various things such as your profiles, favorite books, blog feeds, etc.

- Write articles and have them distributed via distribution services such as ThePhantomWriter.com, or land a gig writing a column for a magazine or newspaper.

Any of these tools can be used together. For example, on your LinkedIn Profile you can list your other websites and profiles. On your blog you can list your other profiles. This allows visitors of any site to visit the other pages where they'll likely find different information, and learn more about you. Having a presence and strategy in various environments might help you connect with others in a place where they feel comfortable. It also builds credibility with the search engines to the point where your pages may get higher rankings in the search engines (that is, you'll show up higher in search results). This is a very simple, incomplete generalization about Search Engine Optimization. You can enter "SEO" in your favorite search engine to learn more.

There are various contact management systems that you can use to manage the relationships you develop on LinkedIn. Just as recruiters will always need their own Applicant Tracking System to make notes on candidates, and salespeople will always need a Customer Relationship Management tool to manage prospects and clients, you should use a relationship management tool to keep better tabs on your relationships.

Your relationship management tool could be as rudimentary as an Excel spreadsheet (good luck!), as complex as a salesperson's contact relationship management suite, or as simple and common as Microsoft Outlook's Contacts section. It should be something you have control over, with the features you need.

Traditional CRM tools include ACT!, GoldMine® and Salesforce.com. Another tool, JibberJobber.com, was designed by my company specifically for managing personal relationships in a career management context—so anyone interested in "climbing the ladder," creating "job security," developing and nurturing a professional network would find JibberJobber.com to be useful. No matter what you use, you should use something.

Another resource is the MyVirtualPowerForum Yahoo! Group. There are thousands of networking enthusiasts that share ideas, resources, tips, frustrations, questions and even contacts and job leads with one another. Originally it was called My LinkedIn Power Forum, and focused on LinkedIn stuff, but it has since expanded its focus to include other social networking tools and networking and professional relationships in general. I've participated in these forums since 2006 and have learned and connected in ways that could only be done through an active email forum. My participation has been an incredible value-add to my LinkedIn networking strategy.

While other social network sites have different features, I doubt any social network is going to completely replace all of the software and tools you use. Make sure you have the proper mix of tools that is right for you. Determining what is right for you might depend on your objectives. Are you:

- Trying to expand your network within your country?

- Trying to expand your network internationally?

- Looking for a forum to voice your opinion and develop your personal brand?

- Looking for a place to learn from other like-minded professionals?

LinkedIn adds new features regularly. Whether it is a change to the front page, the Answers policy or sneaking in a new feature, documenting LinkedIn is like trying to hit a moving target. This is one reason why this book is not just a "how-to" guide for using LinkedIn. Hopefully LinkedIn doesn't change so much of the user experience that the technical parts of this book are outdated before the next edition!

There are a number of great resources to keep up with LinkedIn. I'm not the kind of person who likes to read technical documentation so I'm not going to refer you to that. Instead, these are particular websites, blogs, or posts that I think are valuable to follow so you can ensure you keep current with LinkedIn, and new ideas on how to get value out of it.

- The **ImOnLinkedInNowWhat.com** blog - I started this blog last year, to serve as a supplement to the first edition of this book. It has proven to be a great resource where I can flesh out ideas from the book, talk about current issues, fill in some blanks, and respond to reader's questions. You can sign up to get the posts by email or RSS.

- The **LinkedIntelligence** blog[24] - Scott Allen's blog, which he pretty much stopped posting to. However, there are some great posts as he explains techniques and strategies to help us understand how we can get more value out of LinkedIn.

- Guy Kawasaki's **10 Ways to Use LinkedIn** blog post[25] - Guy lists 10, make that 11, ways to use LinkedIn. Reading these ideas helps ensure you have a proper high-level view of the breadth and depth of LinkedIn. Make sure to read the comments, which have some great ideas.

- Guy Kawasaki's **LinkedIn Profile Extreme Makeover** blog post[26] - Guy received preferred treatment from LinkedIn as they guided him through improving his own Profile (which he had been neglect-

---

24. http://www.LinkedIntelligence.com
25. http://tinyurl.com/2fbver
blog.guykawasaki.com/2007/01/ten_ways_to_use.html
26. http://tinyurl.com/2llban
blog.guykawasaki.com/2007/01/linkedin_profil.html

ing). This post points out the specific changes that LinkedIn recommends to his old Profile. Again, make sure to read the comments as there are some valuable insights there.

- The **My Virtual Power Forum** Yahoo! Group[27] - This is a very active discussion forum that talks about networking, with original focus on LinkedIn. There are some very advanced LinkedIn users here as well as newbies, and frequently you'll find great discussions on a variety of topics and breaking news regarding LinkedIn (and other social environments).

- The **Virtual Handshake** book and blog - Scott Allen and David Teten explore networking and relationships through various online mediums. This might be the deepest, most comprehensive resource on the subject and is a must-read for anyone who realizes they need to use the Internet to develop relationships. Download the book for free at http://www.TheVirtualHandshake.com and check out their blog at http://www.TheVirtualHandshake.com/blog.

- The **LinkedIn User Agreement page**[28] - If you are serious about using LinkedIn, you should read this at least once (don't worry, it is short and fairly easy to read). There are a number of violations that would cause LinkedIn to freeze your account so getting familiar with the rules, and philosophies behind the rules, will help keep your LinkedIn strategy inline.

- The official **LinkedIn blog**[29] - This blog has really matured since it first started, and has excellent information and news for LinkedIn users and fans. There are many authors of this blog, so you get a good mix of information, including recent releases, LinkedIn best practices, etc.

---

27. http://tinyurl.com/2tqn6e
finance.groups.yahoo.com/group/MyLinkedinPowerForum/
28. http://tinyurl.com/zl5tl
linkedin.com/static?key=user_agreement&trk=ftr_useragre
29. http://blog.linkedin.com

- The **LinkedIn Notes** blog[30] and tips website[31] - Rick Upton provides a number of thoughts on using LinkedIn that provide bite-sized, consistent value to your LinkedIn experience.

- The **LinkedIn Users Manual** blog[32] - Peter Nguyen has good ideas on making money with LinkedIn, selling knowledge, etc.

- Deb Dib's article **LinkedIn—What It Is and Why You Need to Be On It**[33] - this is an excellent article written for executives in career transition. There are eight links to very compelling LinkedIn Profiles that you must check out as you optimize your own Profile.

- The unofficial **LinkedIn brainshare wiki**[34] - this is a project started by Marc Freedman with the idea of gathering valuable LinkedIn resources, tips, tricks, user experiences, etc. It's definitely worth your time visiting this website to learn more about LinkedIn from someone who has built his business around LinkedIn.

- The **LinkedIn Personal Trainer** is a book by Steve Tylock. Steve wrote this book to help people get started with LinkedIn, and has a bunch of worksheets you can use as you get your LinkedIn strategy up and running. You can find more information at http://www.LinkedInPersonalTrainer.com. Also, in the last year there have been a number of books on LinkedIn hit the market. Simply go to Amazon.com and search for LinkedIn.

- **GetSatisfaction.com** is where you can see current issues and make complaints about LinkedIn (and other companies). Frequently I'm asked how to resolve something, make recommendations, etc. I have had very poor experiences getting replies from LinkedIn employees, and have seen their involvement in LinkedIn forums decline. But they monitor the discussions and complaints at Get-

---

30. http://linkedin-notes.blogspot.com
31. http://tinyurl.com/77dgy
rickupton.com/linkedin-tips.htm
32. http://tinyurl.com/2u3d6x
linkedinusermanual.blogspot.com/
33. http://tinyurl.com/59jtvd
job-hunt.org/executive-job-search/linkedin-for-executives.shtml
34. http://linkedin.pbwiki.com

Satisfaction in an admirable way. If you have something that isn't getting any attention from Customer Service, you could try posting it at http://www.GetSatisfaction.com/linkedin.

In addition to these resources, do not underestimate a solid networking book to learn some networking basics. Online networking and offline networking have one key thing in common—it's all about relationships. Here are some great networking books I recommend:

- **Never Eat Alone**[35] by Keith Ferrazzi - I read this book when I thought networking was all about desperate people schmoozing and passing business cards for self-gain. It really changed my perspective on what networking is and how to do it, and I strongly, strongly recommend it to anyone who asks about networking.

- **Some Assembly Required** and **The ABC's of Networking** by Thom Singer[36] - Thom's books are great resources with hundreds of practical, right-now relationship building tips. While he talks about relationship and networking stuff, I've found his writings to be especially applicable in the corporate environment with a lot of examples on how he enriches customer and prospect relationships. Thom's new books include Some Assembly Required for Women and Some Assembly Required: LinkedIn ("how to make, grow and keep business relationships using online services such as LinkedIn and others").

- **Dig Your Well Before You're Thirsty**[37] by Harvey Mackay - This has been a staple of networking books for a long time. Harvey Mackay has written a number of best-seller books on networking and career management and is definitely an authority in this space.

---

35. http://www.keithferrazzi.com
36. http://thomsinger.com/
37. http://tinyurl.com/2j247k
store.harveymackay.com/SearchResults.asp?Cat=1

- **Jeffrey Gitomer's Little Black Book of Connections: 6.5 Assets For Networking Your Way to RICH Relationships**[38] - I got this book as a gift from the guy who came up with the name JibberJobber, and it's a gift I cherish. I've been asked by multiple people to include this book as a recommendation for the second edition.

There are a number of new websites and blog posts that talk about LinkedIn from a very high, general perspective down to specific techniques and tactics. Use Google Blogsearch (blogsearch.google.com) to see what the current blog buzz is about LinkedIn. While I've listed some of my favorite resources, I'm sure there are other gems out there I haven't come across yet.

Chapter Summary

- Tools to complement LinkedIn include CRM software, discussion forums and other online profile websites.

- Tools to complement this book include blogs, websites, online resources, and other books.

- LinkedIn should be only one facet of your online social strategy.

- Subscribe to ImOnLinkedInNowWhat.com to keep current on LinkedIn issues, news, thoughts, techniques, etc.

---

38. http://tinyurl.com/yvyktp
gitomer.com/Jeffrey-Gitomer-Little-Black-Book-of-Connections-pluL-BBC.html

17 Conclusion

Hopefully you now have a good perspective on how to get the most out of your experience with LinkedIn, from a "how-to" angle as well as a "why should this matter to me" angle.

Here are some parting thoughts:

- Know what you want to get out of LinkedIn (and related technology).

- Use LinkedIn as the tool that it is.

- Explore the goodies such as premium upgrade options, toolbar plug-ins, and other things from LinkedIn to enhance your LinkedIn experience.

- Figure out what other tools can help you with your online objectives.

- Create a strategy to enhance your personal brand (you know, the brand you already have?) and make sure the tools and approach you use will help you execute that strategy.

- Think about career management, whether you are employed or not, happy or unhappy, a business owner or an executive. And think about how these tools can help you execute your career management strategy.

- Realize you can have a network on LinkedIn, but your entire network is not in LinkedIn. Think about how many people you meet at your family reunion who are in your network but are not LinkedIn connections. It probably isn't appropriate for all (or many) of those people to be in your LinkedIn network. Don't forget there are people outside LinkedIn who have valuable relationships with you. Do you have thoughts or ideas for the third edition of this book? Please email me: Jason@JibberJobber.com.

- Sign up to follow new and current topics at ImOnLinkedInNow-What.com.

- If you found this book valuable, consider leaving a review on Amazon.com (hey, if Andy Sernovitz can ask, why can't I??).

LinkedIn is a great tool—but just like the power tool in your garage, it's useless until you learn how it works, and then actually put it to use!

Good luck!

"Take your connections offline. LinkedIn is a great tool, but don't forget that other tools still exist. Your phone still works, and there's nothing better than a face-to-face connection."
-- Scott Ingram, *http://www.NetworkinAustin.com*

"LinkedIn doesn't replace traditional networking; it facilitates it. Always supplement your online efforts with face-to-face networking."
-- Barbara Safani, *http://www.CareerSolvers.com*

"LinkedIn is a great tool, but you need to learn to use it and you have to maintain it to keep it sharp! Take the time to investigate all the features, encourage colleagues and friends to not only join your network but build their own so you can leverage each other's contacts, and schedule LinkedIn activities with yourself—like updating your Profile once a month, answering questions daily or weekly, etc."
-- Deb Dib, *http://www.ExecutivePowerCoach.com*

LinkedIn for Job Seekers

How can job seekers use LinkedIn in their job search? The same way a salesperson uses LinkedIn: finding new contacts, doing research on them, contacting them, doing company research, etc. Here are 11+1 ways a job seeker can use LinkedIn in their job search:

1. **Fix Your Profile.** Your Profile should NOT say "please hire me, I'm desperate." It should say "I'm a professional, I bring value to my employer and customers." Make sure your Profile is pristine, with NO typos, no grammar issues, and no noise. Kraft your summary, and every letter and word in your Profile, so you come across as the professional you are. Remember, you are a professional in transition, not a job seeker who wants to be a professional. Right?

2. **Search for your Target Companies.** Target Companies are the 5–7 companies you are focusing on. These are the companies you really want to work for. Search for them and find out who is in your network that have ever worked there, as well as what key employees are there and how active they are in LinkedIn.

3. **Grow your Network strategically.** Find people who would have contacts in your Target Company, and invite them to connect. I would do that OUTSIDE of LinkedIn, and work on developing a real relationship with them. Invite them to lunch, ask for an informational interview, or call them on the phone, to get more information about opportunities, other people to contact, etc. As you add contacts from your Target Companies, you'll be able to get better results in your searches.

4. **Browse through your key contacts to look for professional or industry leaders to connect with.** Ask for an Introduction, and try to start a relationship with these leaders. You should continue to network deeper, asking "who do you know who..."

5. **Use the Advanced Search page.** Search for contacts with the job titles you are applying to. Search for contacts who do, or ever have, worked at your Target Companies. Search for contacts who have key titles in industries you are looking for, contacts who are in certain geographic areas, etc. Find these contacts and work on contacting each of them as you grow your network, and look for people who can give you information you need for your job search.

6. **Ask Questions on a regular basis.** The purpose of your questions is to establish your brand with your network. Don't ask questions that can be interpreted as "I need a job, can you help me?" Instead, ask questions that help develop you as a subject matter expert or thought leader. As your network learns more about you, and what you do (or want to do), they'll be in a more prepared situation to help you.

7. **Answer Questions on a more regular basis.** The purpose of answering Questions is the same as asking Questions, however when you answer Questions you get the added benefit of communicating your brand in front of *other people's networks*. Your Answers MUST be value-add, informational, and on-brand. As you answer appropriate questions, appropriately, you should see some new invitations to connect.

8. **Ask for Introductions.** When you find someone you want to network your way into, or connect with on LinkedIn, use the Introductions tool. You will help your First Degree contacts understand what kinds of contacts you want to talk with, AND what your mes-

sage is to them. Make sure you write your Introduction Requests concisely, and with a compelling message, and both parties will learn more about you.

9. **Browse the Network Updates to see who you can reach out to.** You are connected with dozens, or hundreds, of professionals. You need to communicate with them. Too many times I see people not communicating with their LinkedIn Contacts, and they are missing rich opportunities to nurture relationships, communicate brands (see a recurring theme?), and be in the right place at the right time. (Network Updates are found on your home page)

10. **Use the job search tool to find out who else to network into.** I am not discouraging you from formally applying, but the real value of the Jobs section is that you can see who you know in companies that have open opportunities. Apply, but continue to network.

11. **Find Groups to join to expand your reach.** Look for Groups that would have people in your profession, industry, target companies, or even cities or states as members. This will expand your search results and reach, and possibly give you opportunities to communicate with Group members in bulk (depending on how Group Discussions evolve).

Bonus Idea: Share your LinkedIn knowledge with others at job clubs and networking groups. Become that professional in transition who shares tactics and techniques with the other job seekers, who usually have the deer-in-the-headlights look. They will be ever grateful to you for sharing your knowledge, and you'll set yourself someone who believes in givers-gain. And, as you teach, you'll learn more about LinkedIn. This is the only suggestion of these ten that requires you to get out and talk with other people. Don't hide behind the technology!

B LinkedIn for Sales Professionals

Sales professionals can definitely use LinkedIn to increase their network, learn about prospects, do research for sales opportunities, and communicate with decision makers. Here are 10 suggestions for sales professionals to optimize LinkedIn:

1. **If your profile isn't complete, I might not trust who you are when you reach out to me.** Flesh it out with relevant information that helps me learn about you, and maybe even trust you.

2. **Search is your friend.** List some keywords your target segment would have in their profile, including position/role, company, industry, interests, associations, etc. Go into the Advanced People Search page and do various searches using advanced search strings. Get Shally's Cheatsheet so you get the best out of LinkedIn's search functions.

3. **Grow your network shamelessly.** Okay, I mean that tongue-in-cheek, as I won't tell you to blindly add people to your network. But if you want to use LinkedIn for sales, it will make sense to have a very large network. I'm not talking hundreds of first de-

gree contacts, I'm talking thousands. Don't agree with me? Fine, move on to #4, as that will likely make more sense for you (if #3 doesn't make sense, and it shouldn't make sense for everyone).

4. **Grow your network strategically.** Do you sell stuff in one industry? You should amass contacts from that industry. Don't worry about the title. A receptionist in your target industry might have excellent contacts, don't you think? Also, target contacts from adjacent industries, as they should have contacts in your target industry. Your growth strategy could also include certain types of professionals (accountants & CFO's, for example), or professionals in a certain geography, if your target audience is geographically based.

5. **Ask for introductions from your connections.** When you do searches, make sure to include your first degree contacts as you reach out to prospective contacts. As you do this you'll put your brand and messaging top-of-mind with your first degree contacts, and as they agree to help you you'll strengthen your relationship with them. Make sure to nurture individual relationships so you don't just take-take-take in the relationship.

6. **Fill in downtime when you are on the road.** When you get on the road and will have time for a breakfast, lunch, dinner, or other meeting, go into LinkedIn and do a mile radius search. Use the keywords to try and narrow your potential meetings down to the right people, whether you narrow by job title, etc. Consider hosting a LinkedIn get-together and inviting as many LinkedIn people as you can for dinner. Search Yahoo Groups to see if there is an active Group (Cincinnati, Chicago, etc. have active groups), and promote the dinner there.[39]

7. **Ask questions your target audience would be interested in.** As they read the question, or at least your profile, they should know you are in sales, so don't try to hide that. Be genuine, and ask questions that either they can answer, or they would want to know the answers to. You want to be known as a thought leader,

---

39. http://tinyurl.com/6r5k3e
jibberjobber.com/blog/2007/05/08/using-linkedin-
to-fill-out-your-business-trip

and/or a subject matter expert, and/or a connector in their space, and asking questions regularly could help increase brand awareness for you and your company.

8. **Answer questions your target audience would be interested in.** Sometimes it might be easier to do this, since you don't have to think of new questions on a regular basis. Think about how others will perceive you based on your answer. Answer comprehensively, kindly, and with expertise. Share information and recommend other experts, including your customers and prospects. Get questions asked in Answers via RSS, so you learn about opportunities to chime in without even logging in to LinkedIn.

9. **Join Groups where your audience is, or where their contacts are.** Participate in Group Discussions, but more importantly, browse through Group members to look for contacts to add to your network and communicate with. Send Group Members Inmail messages with clear, concise messaging—focus on the relationship but let them know why you want to connect and what you have in mind.

10. **Set up the RSS feed so you get Network Updates delivered to you as soon as possible.** Reach out to your Contacts as they have news, congratulating them on accomplishments, asking them about changes, commenting on new connections, etc. Use the Network Updates as an opportunity to reconnect and further brand yourself.

11. **Consider advertising on LinkedIn.** Their new advertising feature gives you the ability to choose certain types of LinkedIn users. It's comparatively expensive, but the ads go in front of a demographic that is supposedly above average in regard to income, professional status and decision-making power.

Appendix B: LinkedIn for Sales Professionals

About the Author

Jason Alba is the job seeker and networking advocate. He got laid off in January 2006, just a few weeks after Christmas. Even though he had great credentials and it was a job-seeker's market, Jason could hardly get a job interview. Finally he decided to step back and figure out the job search process, including trying to understand all of the available resources. Within a few months he had designed a personal job search tool, JibberJobber.com, which helps professionals manage career and job search activities the same way a salesman manages prospects and customer data.

Author

Create Thought Leadership for your Company

Books deliver instant credibility to the author. Having an MBA or Ph.D. is great; however, putting the word "author" in front of your name is similar to using the letters Ph.D. or MBA. You are no long Michael Green, you are "Author Michael Green."

Books give you a platform to stand on. They help you to:

* Demonstrate your thought leadership
* Generate leads

Books deliver increased revenue, particularly indirect revenue:

* A typical consultant will make 3x in indirect revenue for every dollar they make on book sales

Books are better than a business card. They are:

* More powerful than white papers
* An item that makes it to the book shelf vs. the circular file
* The best tschocke you can give at a conference

Why Wait to Write Your Book?

Check out other companies that have built credibility by writing and publishing a book through Happy About.

Contact Happy About at 408-257-3000 or go to http://happyabout.info.

Books

Other Happy About® Books

Purchase these books at Happy About
http://happyabout.info
or at other online and physical bookstores.

**I'm on Facebook—
Now What???**

This book will help you come up with your own action strategy to get value out of Facebook.

Paperback $19.95
eBook $11.95

Twitter Means Business

For companies unfamiliar with Twitter, this book serves as a field guide. They will get a Twitterverse tour, and learn about the dozens of firms big and small that have harnessed Twitter as a powerful, flexible business tool.

Paperback $19.95
eBook $11.95

Collaboration 2.0

This book is most beneficial for teams, groups, departments, cross-organizational teams and distributed organizations that are looking at some of the Web 2.0 technologies focused on communication, collaboration and interaction.

Paperback $29.95
eBook $19.95

The Emergence of The Relationship Economy

This book analyzes the factors that are influencing an emerging economy based on the sum of factors driving massive and significant changes to the way everyone will work, play, and live.

Paperback $21.95
eBook $14.95

More Praise for I'm on LinkedIn—Now What???

"'I'm on LinkedIn—Now What???' provides a useful guide for all those looking to better utilize the power of LinkedIn. As Jason writes, LinkedIn is NOT the silver bullet of networking sites; such a site does not exist, and this book does not try to make that point. What this book does incredibly well is show how you CAN use the tool to your advantage; to make connections, to help others, and ultimately, to help yourself! 2 handshakes WAY UP for this great book!"
Phil Gerbyshak, public speaker and author of 10 Ways to Make It Great!

"Jason Alba has established himself as a well-known and widely respected expert in the employment arena. His success in establishing himself and promoting his extraordinary career toolset JibberJobber.com prove that he knows what he's talking about. His understanding of personal branding and networking come together in his new book about using LinkedIn. Authoritative and insightful, this book is a great primer for 'newbies,' yet it's comprehensive enough to offer something of value to even the most seasoned LinkedIn users."
George Blomgren, Talent Acquisition Strategist

"Jason's book is an easy-to-read, well-written, step-by-step tutorial for the novice, or for the person who's already linked in. He reveals his mastery, once again, at making the complex simple, just as he did with his invention of JibberJobber."
Billie R. Sucher, Career Transition Consultant & Author, BillieSucher.com

"You don't have to be a full time social networker to use LinkedIn as a connection making tool and Jason Alba lays this out point by point in 'I'm on LinkedIn—Now What???' where he explains exactly how to use LinkedIn in a way that works for you. A book that I've long needed to explain just what LinkedIn is and isn't to countless friends and clients without buzzwords or hype, it's high on my list of recommendations."
Susan Reynolds, New Media Consultant, ArtsyAsylum.com

"As more and more business professionals hear about LinkedIn, they're looking for a place to go for answers about how to get involved and effectively use this important tool. Jason's book—I'm on LinkedIn—Now What??? is appropriately titled and is the quickest and easiest way to understand what LinkedIn is, it's purpose and how to effectively use it. I'm an avid LinkedIn user and regularly teach classes to busy professionals on how to use it for networking, job search, business development or recruiting. One of the first things I do in all of my sessions is to recommend the book and the companion blog, because there are no other resources out there that cover how to get started and how to effectively use LinkedIn as well!"
Jennifer McClure, Executive Recruiter/Executive Coach,
http://cincyrecruiter.com

"Jason has a great knack of explaining the features and benefits of LinkedIn in a way that doesn't intimidate a novice. Yet he also includes little gems that can benefit even seasoned LinkedIn users. He clearly demonstrates how readers can benefit from LinkedIn in every chapter of "I'm on LinkedIn—Now What???" Readers will understand why they should do something rather than just being told that they should do it. This will bring more value to their LinkedIn experience."
Christine Pilch, Co-owner of Grow My Company and co-author of "Understanding Brand Strategies: The Professional Service Firm's Guide to Growth." http://GrowMyCo.com

"Alba's book is the link you need to power up your LinkedIn results!"
Kent M. Blumberg, Executive and Professional Coach, KentBlumberg.com

"Jason's Personal Brand is consistent in each project he works on, especially in 'I'm on LinkedIn—Now What???' Throughout this book he narrows down exactly what LinkedIn SHOULD be used for so that readers don't confuse it with other social networks. You will encounter information on how to set up your Profile, network through Groups and proper etiquette to use as you grow your LinkedIn database. Jason's thoughtful and honest viewpoint on LinkedIn will teach everyone from youthful professionals to experienced entrepreneurs how to succeed with this tool."
Daniel Schawbel, Publisher, Personal Branding Magazine

Books